Joł

Before the Night Grows Late

the columba press

First published in 2009 by
the columba press
55A Spruce Avenue, Stillorgan Industrial Park,
Blackrock, Co Dublin

Cover by Bill Bolger
Cover photo by the author
Origination by The Columba Press
Printed by Athenaeum Press, Gateshead

ISBN 978-1-85607-646-3

Table of Contents

*To my Redemptorist confrères living and dead
and to the honour of our revered founder,
Alphonsus de Ligouri,
this book is dedicated*

Foreword

Of that unique inner world inhabited by each human person and them alone, the Russian poet, Yvgeny Yevtushenko, wrote:

To each his world is private
And in that world one excellent minute
And in that world one tragic minute
They are private.[1]

In the following chapters it is not my intention to even attempt telling of that private world, that holy of holies which is beyond human capacity to unveil. That excellent minute and that tragic minute must perforce remain ours alone. And yet, it is on the bridge between that private and unique world and the outer world that human interaction occurs and much of life is lived. This book recalls some aspects of what happened on the bridge where my inner and outer worlds touched the inner and outer worlds of others, particularly in the context of my work as a Redemptorist Missioner.

Conscious of living through an age of transition I had often wondered how best to preserve some picture of a way of life that existed less that half a century ago but which the modern mind, even of people in my chosen way of life, find difficult to grasp. Eventually I decided to contextualise it within the framework of my own life as a Redemptorist – a life that had nothing particularly spectacular, nothing to attract headlines, just the life of a foot soldier, a regular missioner, responding and adapting to the death of an old world and the unfolding of a new.

My European Union passport identifies me as an Irish citizen and that is true. I identify myself, however, not simply as Irish but more specifically as belonging to the Gaelic Nation, the Republican Tradition, the Catholic Church and the Redempt-

---

1. Yevtushenko, Yvgeny, 'People' in *Death in Literature* by R. F. Weir, p 42.

orist way of life. This is my pad, so to speak, and from here I am happy to engage with native and foreigner, believer and unbeliever, not arrogating to myself the rightness or superiority of my position but simply stating that this is where I'm at, where I belong, where the me lives and moves and has his being.

I thank all who read the manuscript and offered varied and helpful suggestions, most of which have been adopted. For the book's title I am indebted to Helen Waddell's versification of a Chinese poem. How wonder-full it is that a poet of nigh three thousand years ago can still evoke echoes in the heart.

John J. Ó Ríordáin, CSSR
Mt St Alphonsus
Limerick
Ireland
Christmas, 2008

CHAPTER ONE

Early Years (1936-1950)
My world in the 1940s

The last of six

Although my presence had been sensed and felt for quite some time, my first public appearance was at about half past ten on the morning of Sunday, 22 November 1936 and ever since as the anniversary comes round I am the recipient of birthday cards. My father had just set out for the eleven o'clock Mass in Kiskeam when an excited messenger overtook him with news that he had a son. My arrival caused no little stir and some disbelief in the locality because up to that point our family consisted of five children, all girls. With my arrival there was some assurance of the family name continuing on the O'Riordan farm, an important element in most rural value-systems.

The year of my birth coincided with the grinding poverty of the Economic War in which farmers were worst hit. Whether for that reason or the fact that Nancy was now thirty-six and Jim forty-seven, my parents decided that the family was complete. It was around this time too, 1935 to be exact, that the rhythm method of contraception was discovered. Nancy had two brothers, Denis and Thade Murphy, who were already ordained priests and working in Tasmania. These men were not slow in communicating the new knowledge to their families. Every pregnancy had been life threatening for my auntie Nora Moylan, and another auntie, Peg Bourke in Australia, had died in 1930 while giving birth to her eighth baby. Fortunately, my mother didn't have any such problems nor did she ever have a miscarriage, but the new information was welcome.

There were other blessings too. In our parish of Boherbue and Kiskeam – Kiskeam was the out-church – there hadn't been a mission since 1918 and I often thank God for that because it left people more free to work out how best to manage their relationships and the size of their families. The entire issue of contraception had been highlighted by the publication in 1930 of the encyclical letter *Casti Connubii* (Chaste Marriage) of Pope Pius XI. The missioners were expected to preach the implementation of this letter and they were not wanting in zeal for the task. A saving grace for people in general was the fact that they were solid traditional Catholics and rarely institutionalised. In other words their focus was on the message rather than on the bearer of the message. They respected institutions of church and state but did not identify with them. There was an understanding that one kept a respectful distance from both the clergy and the police. The shortcomings of his ministers did not cause them to deviate from Christ himself. Hence, a row with a priest or a bishop for political, social, religious or other reasons rarely meant a rift with the Catholic Church, although occasionally it might mean undertaking a longer walk to a neighbouring church for Sunday Mass.

Early Memories

What are considered 'early memories' can be notoriously unreliable but I think my earliest memory was of standing up in the cot for the first time. The family were at the supper in the kitchen and I clung to the bars of the cot and managed to get on my feet. At this there was a clap and much rejoicing by my adoring sisters and parents. After graduation from the cot there was a whole kitchen to be explored and one day while thus engaged I had the misfortune to fall on my bottom into a hot frying pan, which was sitting on the open fire. This precipitated howls, tears and hugs of consolation. My sisters hated 'minding the child' and none more so than Anne, a highly intelligent girl and the second eldest. She loved reading and when her turn came for minding she would often tie me to a gate or a bush like a goat while continuing her intellectual pursuits.

It was at this early stage of my career that I gave my first public address at a Sunday Mass in Kiskeam. It cost me no strain at all despite the fact that all my family and relatives were present. Oblivious of the wider public I addressed the celebrant who in those days had his back turned to us and did not fully appreciate the content of the message from his two-years-old parishioner. For such an outburst of premature preaching my parents banned me from church services for a considerable time. While in detention in Knockavorheen, I was aware that another member of the family was staying at home from Mass to mind me; and I remember, too, being able to reach to the level of the kitchen table and hold on to the table top with my fingers.

I remember my sister Eileen trying to explain to me that the Pope was dead. That must have been early in 1939 (the Pope died on 10 February); and some time later, when a record of John McCormack was being played on the radio she had difficulty in convincing me that the man was dead. I don't remember ever being lost as a child but I do remember once being found. There was panic among the family: John had disappeared. The heir apparent was missing. A search conducted around the farm and immediate neighbourhood led to my discovery in a nearby tillage field where I was sleeping contentedly in a cosy sun-drenched niche between drills of beet.

The summer of 1939 was glorious. I can still see my mother and sisters picking buckets of blackberries. I myself indiscriminately stuffed ripe berries into my mouth regardless of the fact that one or other might have a little maggot sitting on it. This amused my sisters who gradually taught me to be a little more discriminating. Many memories of the war years (1939-45) come back to me. I used, for example, go into a tea chest and mimic the radio news, particularly the voice of William Joyce (Lord Haw Haw), 'Germany calling! Germany Calling!' And I do remember with sadness some years later the morning he was hanged by the British.

In the summer of 1939 my uncle, Fr Denis Murphy, was home on holidays from Tasmania but the outbreak of the World War delayed the return to his mission for about a year and a half. It was a difficult time for him. Priests were numerous and neither the local church nor any church within striking distance had work to offer him. Nor did he have an income of any kind. His brother Dan gave him hospitality in the family home (The Shamrock House in Kiskeam) and in return, Denis kept all the relatives supplied with salmon, trout and other fish from the rivers Araglen, Blackwater, Laun and Feale. I can still see those beautiful salmon hanging from the landing on the stairs. Nor can I forget the abundance and taste of the speckled brown trout.

During those years of the war, we had the blackouts. My mother made red curtains with black lining to eliminate every ray of light that might emanate from the home fire or the candle or the lamp. It was fearful to hear the occasional German plane passing overhead. I can still hear the heavy engines and the relief that followed when the sounds had ceased. Among the questions I had for my father was how did the planes stay up and how did they find their way from A to B. The poor man had more things troubling him but he took the time to provide me with explanations that were satisfactory for a three or four year old.

Although not at war, the country was on a war footing described as the Emergency. Many local men were mobilised into quasi militias, the best known being the Local Defence Force (LDF) and the Local Security Force (LSF). My father, having fought the War of Independence and taken the Republican side in the Civil War, now found himself a leader and organiser in a large area west of Kanturk. One night in particular stands out in my memory. Somebody knocking on the door in the middle of the night awakened us. It was the local sergeant of the Garda Síochána. My father got up, hurriedly dressed and left the house with him. Churchill had threatened to invade Ireland and take possession of the ports so there was a full alert. My mother must have been worried sick but I was too young to appreciate the dangers of the situation. The LDF and LSF uniforms consisted of fine outfits of warm clothes and strong brown boots, and even men who only had a passing interest in the antics of Hitler and Churchill signed the dotted line in order to find themselves well clad and shod, perhaps for the first time in their lives.

Growing up in the kind of home that it was, we, the children, had our own military training. It was a way of recreating ourselves with daddy rather than any form of strict disciplinarianism. The sweeping brushes – the kitchen brush and the yard brush – were in much demand as 'rifles'. He would train us to stand to attention, stand at ease, slope arms, and so on. From time to time we would use real rifles too and there was an inviolable law never to point the gun at anybody because 'the devil can load a gun'. This useful piece of folklore was an eminently practical safeguard and more effective than any lectures in logic or morality. At this time too, my father taught me the semaphore system of flag signalling, so important before the arrival of the technological age.

Then there was the rationing. Much talk focused on tea and tobacco. As farmers we were saved from city-type poverty and it was only at second level school in Limerick that I heard of such places as pawnshops. We didn't have much by way of delicacies (e.g. a pot of jam) but we always had potatoes, turnips, cabbage, meat, eggs and plenty of milk. (I can still see the look of astonishment on the guard's face during the census taking when my mother said that we used fourteen pints of milk per day.) On short supply were such items as tea, sugar, white flour and butter. Those farmers who grew sugar beet got a bonus of four stone of sugar from the factory. The black market operated in relation to many things, notably tea and tobacco. I knew a woman who slaved over a washtub all day long for a half-ounce of tea. My father came home one evening and told us how he had met a man who was literally out of his mind for tobacco. The poor man had walked to all the local towns and villages on the basis of a rumour that he'd get something but nothing materialised. My dad could see the crazed look in his eyes and gave him the bit he had himself.

Naturally enough in wartime, there were spies, English ones, German ones, perhaps others. My sister Anne, who was a sharp primary school kid at the time, spoke to a strange man whom she adjudged to be a German spy. As fortune would have it Mrs Neylon, the local teacher in the girls' school and an institution in our community, was scanning the countryside with her binoculars and spotted Anne talking to the stranger. News of the spy did the rounds and next day in school when Anne missed her catechism, Mrs Neylon said, 'You'd know a German spy but you wouldn't know your catechism!' It was around this time that my cousin, Murty Tom Culloty, found a German parachute in the bogs of Meenganine. One or two Germans were on the loose in the area. As far as I know they were eventually arrested and committed suicide by taking poison which they had in their possession.

Fosterage

For reasons unknown to me, the Michaelmas Term of 1943 passed in Kiskeam leaving the junior half of the school without a teacher. In view of this neglect my parents fostered me out to Hanna Culloty, a wonderful saintly widow and a first cousin of my father, who lived in Glencollins Upper. From her home I attended the local school in Ballydesmond, then known as Kingwilliamstown. At Hanna Cullotys I learned much about holiness for the praise of God was ever on her lips and her words were full of gentleness and thanksgiving. Her children, with the exception of Paddy and Seán, had already left the family home, Mary to become a nun, Tommie to join the De La Salle Brothers, and the others to make their way in the world.

One evening after school I was down by the *glaise*. It was in flood and Paddy was fishing. He told me of the eels that lived in the *glaise* and how some of them were very big and might jump out and attack you. Whether he was pulling my leg or attempting to discourage me from going too close to the stream, I certainly kept a safe distance from that stream in future lest the conger eel jump out at me. On 22 November my sister Joan cycled the three or four miles from Knockavorheen to Glencollins bringing me some little treat for my birthday. She was anxious to get home before the dark as rumour had it that guard Bennett had seen a ghost appear at Connell's Cross on the Ballydesmond-Kiskeam road.

When the war ended in 1945 I was eight years old. Johnny Twomey, a near neighbour, walked into the yard and said, 'The War is over.' It must have been the War in the Far East because I was drying my little crop of onions on a sheet of galvanised which I had placed on a hedge in the pump-garden. My next special memory was seeing a photograph in the *Irish Press* of Mr Ghandi's arrival in Dublin. It was probably around that time that we were making hay in the coarse meadows when I spotted Seán Moylan walking towards us in the company of a stranger. It was the artist, Seán Keating, in search of a suitable venue for painting a representation of a Sinn Féin Court. Like artists in general, Keating was going through lean times and Moylan had set out to put some work in his way. My father quickly found him the ideal house (now demolished) in Jack Culloty's of

Knockavorheen, together with as many subjects as he might require for the painting.

Throughout that summer Keating was the guest of Seán Moylan's sister Mamie and her husband Tom Carroll at Moylans shop in Newmarket. My sister Mary Clare was shop assistant there at the time and was impressed by his humble, unassuming manner and simplicity of life. As Keating had no transport, she contacted Jim Bourke who did a daily round in a lorry collecting the butterfat from all the creameries affiliated to the Newmarket Co-op and Jim was happy to give him a lift in the cab. Some other good angel got him an evening lift to Newmarket in the mail-car. Mary Clare and Mamie saw to it that he got his breakfast before leaving and a meal in the evening. During the day he took virtually nothing by way of food despite Peggy Culloty's unstinting hospitality. During his time in Knockavorheen there were some direct benefits to myself and other local children. Post-war scarcity was still a reality and coloured chalks, even the scraps discarded by the big man, were much appreciated by us.

A Political Household

Ours was a political house. The above-mentioned Seán Moylan and my father were not only close friends but had married two sisters, Nora and Nancy Murphy of the Shamrock House, Kiskeam. Both my parents had been active through the War of Independence and Civil War. My father served in the Cork Brigade, first under Terence McSwiney and after his death, under Tomás McCurtain. Then, with the expansion of the Republican Army, Cork formed a number of Brigades and James O'Riordan (my father) became an officer in the North Cork Flying Column under the command of Seán Moylan. During the Civil War he was captured with arms, which carried the death sentence, but while in jail, first in Limerick and later in the Curragh, he managed to conceal his true identity and avoid the firing squad. A few weeks after a sixteen-day hunger strike in the Curragh many prisoners were released and my father returned home, a free man, on 19 December 1923. When he ventured into civilian life and attended a fair in Knocknagree some months later, he had a shootout with the Free State army but after that things settled down apart from a skirmish with the Blue Shirts in the thirties.

My mother was in Cuman na mBan but by lineage was a direct descendant of Tadhg Ó Murchú (Murphy), father of at least eleven sons who fought under Sarsfield during the Jacobite War (1688-91). I know that they were at the defence of Limerick during the Siege of 1691. I'd love to know for certain if they were at the Boyne and Aughrim but the family tradition is not specific beyond the Treaty of Limerick except to say that they joined Sarsfield's army in 1688. A neighbour of theirs, a Crowley man from Knocknaboul, distinguished himself at Aughrim, and if he was there it is likely that his friends and neighbours were in the same unit. After the signing of the Treaty of Limerick two of the Ó Murchú boys, Tadhg Óg and Donal (Donal a' Chogaidh) returned to their father in Ulla near Ballydesmond on Cork-Kerry border. Tadhg Óg was wounded. All the other members of the family went into exile in France in the company of Patrick Sarsfield, their charismatic leader. Under the October skies these tired but undefeated soldiers sailed away from Limerick's towers, down the majestic estuary while flocks of tired wild geese flew in overhead from Nordic lands to winter on the marshes of the Shannon. The family tradition has lost track of our Wild Geese except for the fact that they landed at Nantes. Meanwhile the descendants of Old Tadhg and Donal a' Cogaidh lived on to celebrate their memory. And one such was Nancy Murphy, my mother.

A Reluctant Farmer

To say that my father was a reluctant farmer is probably accurate. Let me hasten to add, though, that he was a good farmer, and an exceptionally good neighbour to 'the widow and the orphan' and there were many such in the immediate vicinity. He was a man for a larger canvas than a hill farm in Sliabh Luachra, and had the Civil War not happened his life would have been in the army.

Like my mother's background, so too did my father's family tradition envelope both sides of the county bounds. His parents and grandparents were natives of Co Cork but had their roots in Kerry. In the mid 17th century, possibly fleeing from the

Cromwellian reign of terror, his mother's people, Cullotys by name, came from Ceapach na Coise near Kenmare to Meentogues in Sliabh Luachra in the company of Eoghan Ruadh Ó Suilleabháin's ancestors. His father's people also inhabited Sliabh Luachra and had land in Glencollins Upper, near Ballydesmond. James, or Jim as he was best known, was a fine raconteur and over the years many a man gave 'I met Jim Riordan' as an excuse for a late homecoming. His formal education didn't go beyond primary, although in those days primary education often continued into the middle and sometimes late teens. As well as being skilled in such rural arts as killing pigs and breaking in horses, he had an excellent memory and a good head for law. He would help people in such matters as the making of wills or the transfer of land or property, and he was also a sound adviser and father figure to a number of young men who had lost their own fathers prematurely.

He was most at home in the world of politics and local history. I can still see him, night after night in the 1940s, dictating the history of the War of Independence in North Cork to my first cousin Richard Moylan, Séan's son, who was my senior by a decade. Whether those notes of Richard still exist I cannot say, but if they do they are good and clear-headed and socially valuable because my father had participated in virtually every military engagement in the region during the entire war effort. Throughout the 1940s and later, monuments were erected in towns and villages all over the Cork-Kerry-Limerick border to commemorate those who had fallen in the fight for freedom. Daddy and I regularly travelled by horse and trap to these events. Paddy McCarthy's in Millstreet stands out in my mind. Paddy was much loved and sorely missed. Other outings included funerals of old comrades in arms, political conventions, Kanturk Show, Newmarket Fete, Millstreet Carnival, Cullen Feis, but, curiously, never a football or hurling match.

When my aunts and uncles visited, which they did with relative frequency, conversation inevitably focused on the Troubles, as the Independence struggle and Civil War were termed. It is no wonder that it did have such a focus for it had all happened within the previous twenty to twenty-five years and their lives, their families, their homes and their livelihood had all been at serious risk. Even after the Civil War was over and my dad was out of jail he was still not safe. Perhaps the shoot-out between himself alone and the Free State Army at Knocknagree fair in the Summer of 1924 was the final act of military hostility in our side of the country.

Conversations on the Troubles also took place outside the church on Sundays. The men would stand on the far side of the road from the chapel gate after the 11.00 am Mass engaging one another in animated conversation peppered with many outbursts of laughter. They chatted as if they hadn't met for years and yet it was a weekly ritual. Reflecting back on it now, I have a better awareness of the fact that looking down the barrel of an enemy gun creates bonds among the survivors. So does excommunication from the church they loved. These joyous laughing friends had experienced both and taken them in their stride.

1947: A Hard Year

The year 1947 was the lowest point in my childhood years. On May Eve a strange man came to visit our house at nightfall. He sat by the fire, made small talk and eventually went his way without giving any clue as to the purpose of his visit. Being a youngster of ten I had gone outside, examined his bicycle and noticed what looked like a shoebox on the carrier. The man belonged to a family who lived several miles away and who were noted for working *piseógs*, that is to say, witchcraft. That winter we lost a number of animals. Our little herd of milch cows grew dangerously low in numbers. One fine in-calf cow fell in the stall and couldn't rise. That was the end for her. One or two more died as well. We wondered about the strange man on the bike. But witchcraft or no, the year was bad. It was unusually wet. Neither turf nor hay was saved. Furthermore, it was the centenary of the Great Famine and I feared another catastrophe when people spoke of the blight on the potatoes that summer.

Despite all the adversity, there came a lovely fine Sunday in early August. After Mass, a local man who owned an open lorry used for drawing turf from the bog took a large group of people, as many as the back of the lorry would hold, to Puck Fair. I remember them setting off in their light summer-wear without coat or jacket, umbrella or hat, nothing but what seemed appropriate to that sun-filled morning.

Well the day changed. It rained and rained and rained as rarely experienced. It rained in Killorglin, it rained in Kiskeam, it rained all over the country and perhaps overseas. The crowd at Puck Fair was drenched, perished, starved. Because of the weather they couldn't go home. Because they were broke or as near as makes no difference they could not find a place to shelter. Finally, they discovered a dance hall particularly patronised by the travelling people. The entrance fee was within their scope and in they went and gladly. As it happened, there was a cousin of mine from Kiskeam who had married into the travelling people, and seeing all his neighbours he rashly concluded that they had come in to laugh at him. The upshot of this false assumption was that he gathered his newfound community together and beat the Kiskeamers out of the premises into the dark night and pelting rain. The lorry arrived home in the middle of the following day and disgorged its famished passengers. When they had dried out, eaten and slept they weren't short of a story to tell.

The Araglen River, normally meandering along without bothering anybody, was spectacular that weekend. The entire valley had become a vast lake. The angry flood coursed down the centre ignoring the winding riverbed that it had carved out over the centuries. Parts of that river were never the same again. The Araglen is a tributary of the Munster Blackwater, a river always beautiful, but on this occasion a spectacle. It, too, broke all boundaries and one man from the Lombardstown side who beheld the sight with terror certainly had a story to tell. He had been out to meet his girlfriend on the Sunday night and got caught in the floods on the way home. If his love was ardent his survival was arduous. If his arms had been tight around his lady they were tighter still around the treetop to which he desperately clung amidst the raging floods until rescued by boat the following day.

A hard winter followed the bad summer. The absence of turf made for difficult cooking conditions. An opportunity came for hiring a lorry to bring turf from the bog on 1 November. That was the Feast of All Saints and a Holyday of obligation. Days such as this were kept with the same reverence as Sunday. In the difficult circumstances in which we found ourselves, Daddy decided to avail of the opportunity of bringing home a lorry load of turf, even wet turf. After Mass he and I and a couple of neighbours set off in the lorry for Glountanefinnane, about ten kilometres into Sliabh Luachra and on the Kerry side of the county bounds. We got there without incident but while the driver was attempting to turn the lorry it got bogged down and try as we might to dislodge them, all through that bitter, wet, miserable day, the wheels of that lorry stayed where they had stuck. Darkness eventually enveloped us and further attempts to extricate the vehicle were abandoned. Disappointed, heavyhearted, starved and drenched, we walked those ten long kilometres home. Two things I remember from that outing: on our arrival home, John O'Leary (John O) from Meentiflugh had eight slices of dry bread eaten while waiting for the kettle to boil; and my father decided that no matter how bad things might be he would never again work on a Holyday.

The winter wasn't all doom and gloom. Because of the weather the school was closed for weeks. Before the closure negotiating snowdrifts in the fields and down 'the long ditch' on my way to school was exciting. Conditions were so bad one day that no teacher and only five pupils turned up. The five of us were first cousins, including John and Con Pat Murphy from the village and two other cousins whose identity escapes my memory. We put down a good fire in the hearth, sat by it, chatted and told stories, ate our lunch at eleven o'clock and went home.

School Days

I have said little about school days. They were not memorable. We all got slapped and physically and psychologically abused but nobody then or since has complained about it. It appeared and still appears as part of the pedagogy of the time. The teachers, male and female, all lay, were products of their time and without exception had their good points as well as their human frailties. In the girls' school my sisters and my first cousins, the Moylans, suffered more than others, particularly when there was a General Election in the offing. Republican families were outcasts in the eyes of some of the teaching staff. I never heard anybody in either boys' or girls' school saying that they loved their teacher. Din-Joe Murphy who taught in the girls' school was an exception: his decency, humanity and all-round goodness were appreciated.

During my primary education, when the 'day of the holidays' came round, the master put away his two-by-one slat of seasoned ash, bought a jar of sweets and after lunch-break called an impromptu concert by inviting pupils to sing a song. Some did so readily and with fine voice. Others, like myself, were shy. Determined to break out of this mould, I bought a broadsheet of *The Old House* from a balladeer at the Pattern in Cullen on St Lateerin's Day and learned the words by heart as I walked the five miles home. On the next 'day of the holidays' when asked to sing, I shot to my feet and gave a rendition of *The Old House*, rather too fast because of nerves, but nevertheless I did it. That memory remains green because whenever I hear that song, it brings me back to the day of the holidays in the old (1847) primary school in Kiskeam where my maternal great grandfather and his brother were the first teachers.

The Shadow of the Blue Shirts

The general election of 1948 saw the defeat of the De Valera government after sixteen years in office. Emotions ran high in our house. There was sorrow at the defeat of Davie Leary, my father's affectionate name for Dev. There was fear of a return of the Blue Shirts who in the previous decade had raided our home more than once and had also violently assaulted my father and split his head. Even my sister Mary Clare, then eight or nine years of age, had to run the gauntlet of taunts and insults when she went to the village for messages. On foot of the election defeat, I remember my father calling a hurried conference in our house at a late hour of the night. Shortly afterwards, again at a late hour, a number of his compatriots returned, collected the seven or eight rifles that were resting inside the casing of my room and placed them in a dump for safe-keeping. There the rifles remained until my father, nearly twenty years later, was persuaded to resurrect them and present them to Kilmainham Jail Museum. They were received on behalf of the museum by the then Taoiseach, Jack Lynch, during Easter Week, 1967. On that occasion, too, my father presented what was probably his most treasured possession, 'the bomb'. I have written about the bomb elsewhere and will not labour it here, but it was a homemade gelignite land mine dating from the War of Independence. It hadn't exploded during an ambush on the British because the wrong detonator had been attached to it. I will always remember Jack Lynch's fascination with the bomb. He was intrigued that the men of the Republican Army could take on the British Empire at its zenith with such crude weapons as that before his eyes – and win!

The Social Milieu of the Forties

The 1940s was the only decade I spent at home apart from my infancy in the late 1930s. In many ways it was the idyllic life once beautifully articulated by De Valera; in other ways it was little more than drudgery, symbolised by wellingtons and cow dung. In spite of the hardship, there was a wonderful natural rhythm to the farming year. With the passage of time one aspect of it in particular fascinates me. It is the mid-winter period. The farming year ran from 1 February to Christmas Eve. Young and not so young men who worked as farm labourers, known colloquially as servant boys, arrived home late on Christmas Eve. Servant girls were less fortunate. Their work never seemed to end. But from Christmas until 1 February the servant boys were free men. There was freedom too for the farmers themselves. Farming was at a standstill except for cleaning out the sheds and foddering and watering the animals. Otherwise it was hibernation or as close as humans come to it. Looking back on it now it all stands in marked contrast to the glare and stress of a consumerist culture.

The high winter was also the time for matchmaking, house dances and impromptu concerts, if one may use the term in relation to singing songs by the fire or playing the fiddle. Both my parents were fine dancers and in due time all my sisters became such, my eldest sister Mary Clare winning prizes for ballroom dancing. It was almost taken for granted that young people would try their hand at playing the fiddle, acquiring the art from their seniors or taking formal lessons from fiddle-masters. Some of those who persevered had fame thrust upon them – my Murphy relatives, Denis the Waver (Weaver) and his sister Julia Clifford, being the best known. My Godfather, Johnny-Billy

Murphy, a descendant of Eoghan Rua Ó Súilleabháin, the 18th century Sliabh Luachra poet, was a splendid fiddler, as were Johnny O'Leary of Dromscarra, Jim Breen of Doonasleen (Jim the Fiddler) and Maurice O'Keeffe of Gleanreagh.

It was Jim the Fiddler's brother, Davie, who gave me my first – and last – lesson in the art. Davie had survived for many years as a busker on the streets of New York. After his return to Ireland he was at a loose end and we gave him free board and lodgings for a winter. He slept comfortably in the loft, unaware that he was sharing it with the above-mentioned rifles. He was welcome to the board and lodgings but my dad had a secondary motive for keeping Davie close at hand. He was aware that casual labour was not readily available in springtime and had in mind hiring Davie when the need arose. One day, in or about February or early March, we were cutting *sciolláns* (seed potatoes for planting). Davie emerged from his snug chamber at his usual hour, not too early, and noted the business atmosphere about the place. He had his breakfast, collected his few belongings and politely said, 'I think I'll be going now, Mr O'Riordan.' So ended his winterage in Knockavorheen and my father's dream of having a helping hand in the spring. The incident became part of the family lore and a cause of much laughter over the years.

During the winter of his residence with us Davie gave me that fiddle lesson. My excitement ran high as the appointed time drew near. When all was ready my tutor made a few introductory remarks as he showed me how to hold the fiddle properly. That went fine. He then set about teaching me how to hold the bow but on discovering that I was left-handed he summarily dismissed me as one of the *damnati*, unworthy of association with the fiddling fraternity.

With my career in the world of strings in tatters, another and more illustrious avenue opened up. Din Kiely admitted me to membership of Kiskeam Brass Band in which body I played a valve trombone. The band itself had come into being in the 19th century during the temperance movement. At an early stage it had been housed in 'The Band Room' in the Shamrock House, but as long as I knew it and for a generation or two previously it was identified with the Kielys, a local family of shoemakers and musicians. The band had a chequered career during the Land

War, the War of Independence and in later times. There was an understanding that under attack, the musical instrument could, and often did, double as a weapon of war. In Din Kiely's words, 'If anyone will attack ye boys, ye have yer instruments.'

Our band was under the patronage of Thomas Ashe, the Lispoleman and 1916 patriot who died of ill treatment in Mountjoy jail on 25 September 1917. To the best of my knowledge Kiskeam was first to honour him and I was always proud to march under the fine banner bearing his image and the questionable inscription, 'One man dead for Ireland is worth a thousand men.'

My Kiskeam childhood ended in 1950 but from the middle of the 1940s it had already begun to unravel. One by one my sisters departed, first for a spell in boarding schools, then for employment. Mary Clare went to St Louis Convent Ramsgrange and then to the Munster Institute; Anne, Peggy, Joan and Eileen followed to Ramsgrange, and Peggy also went for a time to Presentation Convent, Crosshaven. Afterwards, Mary Clare stayed within Munster. Anne and Peggy trained as nurses in England. Joan focused on hotel work in Dublin, while Eileen and I stayed at home a little longer.

Having grown up on a farm in the 1940s all the girls were determined not to marry farmers, nor did they, with the exception of Mary Clare. Anne married in San Francisco and moved to New Zealand. Joan married in Dublin and later moved first to London and then to Limerick. Peggy married in Cork where she had been nursing but her talent and vocation might have been more completely fulfilled as a medical doctor. Eileen, too, in her own time, moved out and worked first with Joan in Dublin, and later with Anne in New Zealand, before returning in 1963 to remain with my ageing parents in Knockavorheen.

CHAPTER TWO

The Juvenate (1950-1955)
A Redemptorist minor seminary

The Mission

There was a Redemptorist Mission in our parish in 1948, the first remembered mission or retreat of any kind in thirty years. People flocked to it. The missioners were Fathers Patrick Whelan and Michael Hickey with a short appearance put in by Harry Potter. Harry, a chaplain in the Great War, had been awarded the Military Cross for bravery and was now on the parish mission staff in Limerick. Of the three, Fr Michael Hickey was the star performer, so to speak. Still in the prime of life, he was a fine preacher, an accomplished communicator, a veteran of our Philippine mission and tense with the tension of a thoroughbred.

Missioners need a pulpit and Kiskeam had none. My uncle Paddy Joe Murphy, a gifted man with his hands, was called to the rescue and in no time at all had a brand new pulpit made to the preachers' specifications – a designer pulpit if you will. It was to last for many years because if it survived Michael Hickey it was not going to succumb to lesser mortals. Well satisfied with their new platform, the missioners launched into their work. Each person who went to Confession received from the missioner a small souvenir leaflet bearing an image of the Crucified Christ on the front together with the name of the parish, the date of the mission and the fact that it was being conducted by the Redemptorist Fathers.

The remaining three pages were filled with short basic prayers and instructions which were part of the mission tradition from the 19th century – acts of contrition, faith, hope and charity; a reminder that one had only one soul to save, one God to love, and heaven or hell as an ultimate destination. To avoid the latter, there were further recommendations in relation to Christian lifestyle and there was a particularly sobering one to be prayed before sleep. It recommended that having got into bed each night, one ought to fold one's arms in the form of a cross and say, 'I must die, I know not when nor how nor where, but if I die in mortal sin, my soul is lost for ever.' There were no hymn books but the missioners taught us each morning and night, line by line, repeat, repeat, try it again, and after two weeks we ended up with a substantial repertoire and a full-voiced congregation.

At the time of the mission I was an altar server and all of us servers felt particularly important as we had full employment late and early for two weeks, whereas in normal circumstances there was only one Mass on a Sunday in which to display our liturgical awareness and linguistic competence, at least as far as answering the Latin Mass was concerned. Fr Hickey might have been happy enough to be rid of us off the altar during the evening mission if we were to judge by his glower when little feet were shuffling. Nevertheless, it was during that mission that the idea of my becoming a missioner myself was born.

A Lay Church
Despite the absence of parish missions and other services that are taken for granted in many churches, the faith was strong among us and our community was rich in vocations to both the priesthood and religious life. In the local parish we had four priests in the presbytery in Boherbue. One of them came to celebrate Mass in Kiskeam at eleven o'clock on Sunday. Other than that appearance we rarely saw a priest except on a visit to the school or at a funeral Mass if there was one. With the exception of the Sunday Mass the Catholic community, and we were all Catholics, somehow looked after itself. If somebody died the neighbours rallied round for the wake. As often as not, Mrs Neylon, a local teacher, laid out the body, and if the remains were brought to the church, it was the same Mrs Neylon who received them and said the Rosary and the Litany of Loreto and a few trimmings.

To my knowledge, nobody felt deprived or neglected by the fact that none of the four priests in the parish had called to the house or been present at the removal to the church. As I said in the previous chapter, the people were not institutionalised and knew how to handle and pass on the faith they had inherited by the grace of God. Every home had daily family prayer, almost always the Rosary. It was only when I got to college in Limerick that I came to realise that this was not the regime in every home in Ireland. Apart from sacramental life, the community did not depend on the priest for the celebration of their life in Christ. At the same time, a vocation to the priesthood was highly appreciated and in my mind's eye I can still see neighbours praying in the chapel and I knew that they were praying for me.

In Kiskeam the priest was certainly the acknowledged spiritual leader of the community, but there were boundaries he might not pass. As I reflect on the Catholic Church in Kiskeam in the first half of the twentieth century, I think of my father and Seán Moylan putting manners on a curate whose tongue was too loose at a Station Mass in Knockavorheen. He referred to the Republican Army as 'bastards'. On the way home, Seán and Jim held him up at gunpoint. The poor man was terrified, relieved too, no doubt, when they said, 'We won't shoot you but remember that we are not bastards.' Then, there was the Sunday when Moylan interrupted the parish priest in the course of his sermon with the corrective, 'Stop your politics and preach the gospel.'

In Knocknagree, five miles away, Mr Herlihy, a member of the Irish Republican Brotherhood, was on that account publicly refused Holy Communion at the altar. That did not turn him from the faith. As a matter of fact, he had three sons who became priests and one of those became president of the Irish College in Rome and later a bishop in Ireland. And I think I was actually present myself when our own parish priest called on my father at Sunday Mass to apologise to somebody and Jim shouted up to him, 'I will not, nor to you either Father!' Whether my father ought to have apologised or not is irrelevant here. The point I'm making is that these men and others like them were independent-minded and uninstitutionalised; and if sinners, then firmly committed Catholic ones.

Vocation

It was as an altar server that I first felt the desire to be a priest. At that time I was about ten years of age and had no idea of distinctions between secular priests and religious orders. The local parish priest, Fr David Breen was a good man who had the welfare of his people at heart. He did much for the parish that had been so neglected for years and was well loved by the community. Fr Breen had a feel for the Latin, too. He relished the strong rhythm of the 13th century hymn *Dies Irae*, recited at all Masses for the dead, and almost smacked his lips at the cadences. The people did not know what he was saying to God but were readily aware that it was serious stuff.

Quaerens me, sedisti lassus:
Redemisti crucem passus:
Tantus labor non sit cassus.[1]

One of the tasks assigned to a senior boy was to make the fire and boil the kettle for the master's lunch. While so engaged one day, the master, Mr O'Connor – locally known as Jackie-Andy – asked me what I had in mind doing with my life. A lot of my contemporaries would have been thinking of going to Oregon or to England or to work for farmers. I said that I'd like to be a priest. Things rested so until early in 1949 when there came to our school a Redemptorist missioner named John Duggan. He was not on a mission this time but looking out for recruits, a vocations director. The Master must have tipped him off during a chat at the rostrum because he singled out yours truly, a scrawny streak of misery head and shoulders over the rest and, placing his biretta on my head, flatteringly remarked 'You'd make a fine Redemptorist.' And with that he had another catch in his bag, the easiest vocation he ever recruited.

The plan was that I would go to the Redemptorist College in Limerick for secondary education, starting in late August. It was all too much for my mother. She was starting the change of life and the thought of having to cope with seeing her youngest child leave home, together with the problem of finding the money and fulfilling all requirements of clothes, shoes, sports gear and the rest, was a tall order at short notice. After some further consultation it was agreed that I'd postpone departure for a year and go in August 1950, which I did.

The idea of his only son abandoning the family farm in favour of following a religious vocation brought some of the

---

1. Faint and weary, you have sought me,
   On the Cross of suffering bought me.
   Shall such grace be vainly brought me?

values most cherished by my father into sharp conflict. We had been two centuries or more on that land and he loved it, not merely for its own sake only but because this was the land worked by his relatives and ancestors and had provided them with sustenance even through the bitter years of the Great Famine and far beyond. And being a man steeped in the rural tradition, relinquishing the family name on the property further aggravated matters. On one occasion he did ask in a sort of musing fashion what he would do with the family farm in the event of my joining the Redemptorists. Insensitively, I simply replied, 'Plant it!' The response arose out of an article on reaforestation which had impressed me but I always regret having said it because it must have further added to the pain he was already feeling.

But James O'Riordan also loved and respected his church, despite its ministers' occasional frowns or at times outright opposition. He therefore never raised an objection to my choice, facilitated me in every way and kept his thoughts to himself. On my three days' leave after ordination some of the neighbours told me how sad and low of spirit my father was for years after my going; and then, as ordination approached, he picked up again becoming his usual self.

For a farmer's youngster to leave home in late August was no mean sacrifice. It wasn't simply a matter of leaving father and mother and family and friends and neighbours. That was bad enough. But it meant leaving the ripening grain and no longer being free to contemplate the wonder of a harvest moon rising gloriously over the stubbles and stooks of corn. It meant that my ears would no longer pick up the distant hypnotic hum of a threshing machine in the autumn air.

Denis (Mike-Seán) Cronin from Dromscarra Cross was already a student at Redemptorist College and he shepherded me along on my first journey. Coming from Limerick Station to the college we passed through the People's Park and as we walked Denis entertained himself by trying to persuade master greenhorn that it was all part of the college grounds. On that journey from the station I got my first glimpse of the Shannon and we sheltered from the rain at Dick Quin's Garage in Henry St. That afternoon we went to the cinema. Whether it was the Savoy or the Carlton I cannot say. I guess either would have had the same effect on me as it was my first time setting foot in such an establishment, although I had seen a few films courtesy of the travelling companies who set up their tent in the Lawn in Kiskeam from time to time. By contrast with the wooden seats in the Lawn, the luxury of a cinema was no small culture shock. I think the film was *Lydia Bailey* and was located somewhere among the scary swamps of Alabama or along the Gulf of Mexico.

The College

A Redemptorist second-level college and minor seminary was established in Mt St Alphonsus, Limerick in 1884. Among ourselves this college was termed the Juvenate, a word ultimately derived from Juventus or Juventas, a Roman goddess who presided over youth and vigour and was represented as a beautiful nymph. Nobody told us of this derivation of Juvenate. Not only that, there was a strict injunction not to consort with nymphs. The original Juvenate was incorporated into the monastery, but with the growth of numbers aspiring to join the Congregation, a new college was built in 1936. It was named St Teresa's by a provincial superior whose devotion to the saint of Avila exceeded his common sense in so naming a second-level boys' school. After his death it was renamed St Clement's College and in the interim it was simply known as the Redemptorist College or the Juvenate.

When I arrived in the Juvenate in 1950 the student population was sixty. Two or three years later the college was extended to its present physical dimensions (except for the science block) in order to cater for one hundred. We were all boarders, all desiring to be Redemptorist priests. If it happened that anywhere along the way between first year and Leaving Certificate a student had a change of mind, they were also expected to have a change of school. In such circumstances they would be allowed to finish out the term but not the year. Other aspects of the regime in the college ran on the same strict basis and it was all a far cry from the freedom of Knockavorheen. We rose at 6.20 am. Morning prayer followed. Then in succession: Mass, study, breakfast and remission – a well-chosen word with its echoes of bolts and bars.

Games were a feature in all colleges and the Juvenate was no exception, although in my early years we were not allowed to participate in inter-college matches. For myself I never had much interest in games. They generally bored me to tears. And no one will be surprised to learn that I was useless at them anyway. Later in life I was to discover that I should never have been playing in the first place because of a heart condition.

If games were not the thing for you, then it was walks, and bad and all as games might be, walking was as bad or worse. Apart from the boredom of walking in procession, two by two, through dull streets, passing sweet shops that we dared not enter, and trying to make small talk with a companion, I frequently returned with painful neuralgia. Manual work in the garden was better although it was too restricted to be really enjoyable. I had been used to sowing, planting and all aspects of efficiently cultivating a simple kitchen and flower garden since childhood.

The fine vegetable gardens, orchards, flower gardens and greenhouse in the college and monastery grounds impressed me. I had never seen the like – flowers and vegetables and plants which did not grow in Sliabh Luachra, or if they did, certainly not in Knockavorheen. These gardens and orchards were our recreation grounds when we were not engaged in field sport or out for a walk. Recreating oneself in these surroundings was no easy task after summer holidays. In fact having remission in the garden was tantamount to an invitation to relax in a torture chamber. There we were, ever hungry as youngsters tend to be, walking about this garden, ducking our heads to avoid bumping into trees laden with apples, pears and plums, and at the same time watching our steps lest we stand on any fruit that had fallen to the ground. There was the large greenhouse, too, with its fruitful vines bearing an abundance of beautifully formed bunches of red and green grapes. There was an iron discipline in force. If a student was caught taking a fruit, even off the ground, the penalty was expulsion. I did five years of this without a fault and I guess most others did the same. It was probably meant to be good training for self-control in later years but I'm not sure about its effectiveness.

Although we might have wished for more food at times, our

college was rated better than most similar institutions of the day. Fr Gerry Carroll, a humble, kindly man, was forever foraging on our behalf, be it buying the contents of orchards out the country or managing to get honey or some other little treat for us.

The Staff

The college staff consisted of domestic staff and the teaching faculty. The only layperson on the domestic staff was the gardener and the teaching faculty consisted wholly of Redemptorist priests with the exception of the music and gymnastics instructors. During the first days in class it became evident that there was no slapping of pupils. This was good news and a welcome change from primary school in Kiskeam where the master dexterously wielded a two-by-one planed slice of ash. Nevertheless there were other ways and means of punishing. Teachers can be creative and inventive in that regard. Kneeling for lengthy periods or writing so many times on the blackboard were standard punishments, but some teachers had more sophisticated techniques, both physical and psychological.

It was especially in the early stages of my secondary education in the college that I was frequently ill and tended to catch every cold and flu that was going. During those days I came to know the wonderful kindness of three Redemptorists on the domestic staff, Brother Basil, Brother Bartholomew (Bart) and Brother Tom Farrell (Virgilius). All three were young, not much over twenty years of age and full of goodness. In later years Brother Tom Farrell was my confrère in Esker monastery and the goodness that he displayed in the days of his youth hadn't diminished a whit nor had his delightful sense of humour and spirit of prayer.

The Curriculum

The curriculum was simple and solid. Irish, English, Latin, Greek, French, Maths, History and Geography were standard, while piano tuition was available as an elective. Non-exam subjects included apologetics, singing and music appreciation. The college director, Fr Tom McKinley, who had a keen appreciation of good vocal and instrumental music, tried with some success to pass it on to the rest of us. We were introduced to the voices of

Jussi Björling, Beniamino Gigli and Enrico Caruso but I cannot remember any introductions to some of their female counterparts, the soaring soprano voices of Elizabeth Swartzkopf, Amelita Galli-curci and Nellie Melba. McKinley allowed us attend some classical concerts in town, including a performance by the Hallè Orchestra under the baton of Sir John Barbarolli. On a less highbrow level and despite being few in number – there were only sixty in the Juvenate in my early days – a Gilbert and Sullivan opera was produced and performed in the college each year. This had the twin effect of ensuring that as many as possible had exposure to appearing in public on stage while anyone with a note in his head could sing the arias from several of the operas, if not on stage, at least in the shower.

We sat examinations three times a year, house-exams at Christmas and Easter, state exams in summer. Before the summer examinations we made a walking pilgrimage (fourteen miles round trip) to the Lourdes Grotto in Cratloe Wood. There we recited the rosary, ate our sandwiches, had some free time and returned home. There were always casualties on this trip, people got bad blisters or other ailments and, as far as I can recall, it was only once that I completed the round trip on foot.

In the college we received a considerable amount of spiritual and moral formation. There was the daily routine of morning and night prayer and the Mass. It was in the Juvenate, too, that I was introduced to devotion to the Mother of Perpetual Help, although the picture was already familiar since it hung in our kitchen since my mother married into Knockavorheen. We had a three-day silent retreat in September, another in Holy Week and one day before Christmas. Besides, the director of the college gave two public talks per week and each of us received personal spiritual direction from him at regular intervals.

Although almost nothing distinct remains in my conscious mind from those retreats and lectures, they had their formative influence. There is, however, one quotation from an early retreat, probably given by Fr Eddie McHugh, which stayed with me. It ran, 'If you want to be a good Redemptorist you must be able to eat well, sleep well and pray well.' The sentence was delivered in solemn tones. The key words, eat, sleep and pray, were each stressed while his elongation of the vowel in *práy* thus rounded off the sentence with a fine flourish.

It would be untrue to say that I liked being in the college. I didn't. It was a lonely place for a country lad who loved land and cattle and trees and bogs, but for whom games held no interest. We were in bed while the world around us was up and about. We were up when the world still slept. There was a particularly trying period of study on Sunday afternoons. We were expected to work on maths or Latin and Greek verbs while our ears were bombarded by the shrieks and screams coming from across the wall where the Laurel Hill girls contested their hockey matches. It is little wonder that down the years as a missioner I have saved many a young person from being sent boarding.

In my own situation, however, there was no second-level school within daily striking distance of my home. Two or three of my hardier contemporaries cycled every day to Newmarket or Kanturk, but for all the rest schooling ended with the Primary Certificate. If I wished to be a Redemptorist priest I had to get secondary education somewhere, so why not in the Redemptorist College which was established specifically for that purpose.

'College Training'

Since I was one of the very few local lads who had the privilege of getting secondary education, and fewer still had ever been in a boarding school, great things were expected of me in the playing fields of Kiskeam. I was scarcely home in first year when I was eagerly sought out by the local team. I always remember playing down in the field in front of the chapel one afternoon and whatever way I got possession of the ball and kicked it, it impressed another young fellow on the sideline. 'College training,' I heard him say. But it didn't take the Kiskeam boys long to learn that college training or no, they had a useless footballer on their hands and they allowed me to find my proper place – on the sideline or down on the farm.

There is something else that I remember and haven't ever forgotten. On returning from my first term in college I was carpeted by Con-Tim Murphy, a local shopkeeper for saying 'Oh, shag!' 'Shag' happened to be the current expletive in college at the time and nobody there seemed to see any problem with its use. However, my naïve appeal to 'coarse tobacco' cut no ice with the worldly-wise Con-Tim. In my native Kiskeam, 'bad language' although used at times by some, was not acceptable.

Shortly before sitting for the Leaving Certificate there were local elections in the offing and the Fianna Fáil Cumann, anxious to keep a youthful image, invited me to introduce their candidate, Danny-Martin Murphy of Glounakeel, Rockchapel. It involved standing on the back of a lorry and without amplification addressing the gathered Kiskeam community after Sunday Mass – a far cry from my unsolicited intervention in church at the age of two. Nevertheless, when the opportunity beckoned, I accepted. In view of my imminent departure for the Redemptorist novitiate, Cicero's 'I have not chosen the political avenue of life' provided me with a suitable entrée. Of what followed I have no memory except that Danny-Martin won a seat, having failed on a number of previous occasions, and I tried to convince myself that his election was not entirely due to my few hurried words off the back of the lorry.

Love & War

While in primary school, at the age of nine or ten, I fell in love with a little girl whose raven hair fell around her pretty face in a shower of curls and ringlets. As with Dante and Beatrice, this attraction did not fade and about half way through my secondary schooling, as the summer holidays drew to a close, I said to my mother, 'I don't think I want to be a priest any more.' She must have been both taken aback and disappointed but didn't show it, and calmly replied, 'That's all right, but you'll have to do a couple of years in the army anyway.' Well, with the sound of those words my vocation suddenly returned with such force that I never looked back, because for me at least, if there was one state worse than being in love, it was being in the army.

Down the years I often thought about that incident and wondered if indeed I had joined the Redemptorists for the wrong motives and perhaps had no true vocation. By the goodness of God everything fell into place a few years ago when, having entertained the confrères with the story of my vocation and my brush with the army, Stan Mellett remarked, 'Well, your subsequent life has clarified that anyway.' That simple comment came to me as a kind of confirmation of my whole life – a sacrament.

I finally left the college having completed the Leaving Certificate and as I closed the big iron gate for the last time, a lump came to my throat and a tear to my eye. No, I had never loved the place, but I had somehow integrated the various experiences of my five years there and was ready to move on.

CHAPTER THREE

The Novitiate (1955-1956)
A novice hurdle

The Summer of 1955 was glorious. I lay on the beach in Ballybunion until I was virtually indistinguishable in colour from the sand. There was one snag. I had to be in the novitiate in Esker on 20 August, the feast of St Bernard. The novitiate introduced aspirant religious to the way of life they were about to adopt. It has taken various forms over the centuries and is in the process of change again as I write, but in the 1950s one might legitimately describe it in racing terms as a novice hurdle. If you survived the novitiate you were home and dry, safely through to profession as a Redemptorist even though priesthood would not follow for another six or seven years. There are of course, Redemptorists who never get ordained because we are primarily a brotherhood and within that some find their full vocation as members of the brotherhood while others have the call to priesthood as well. The Irish language is more attuned to this: all members of a Religious Order, cleric or lay, are *na bráithre*, the brothers.

Founded by Cromwell
In my time, the novitiate was in Esker Monastery, famous for being, as one confrère put it, founded by Oliver Cromwell. Not that the good gentleman took a personal hand in its establishment, rather did the Cromwellian persecution lead to the final abandonment of the Dominican Friary in Athenry and those brothers who had not been killed or gone into exile survived by hiding in the bogs and woods of Esker, about four kilometres east of the town. There they and their successors lived, secretly ministered to the people, and recruited and ordained new members until more peaceful times returned. Then in 1891 the Dominicans who had first come to Athenry in 1241 left of their own volition and gifted their foundation in Esker to the diocese

of Clonfert. A decade or so later the Redemptorists bought it as a centre for missions in the West of Ireland and so it has remained to this day.

Esker was remote in the days of Cromwell and had he been there in 1650, I'm fairly certain that he would still be able to negotiate his way around three hundred years later, because in 1950 Esker was still remote. To us it was 'the bog' and a world of entertaining Redemptorist folklore has grown up around it – tongue-in-cheek references to detention, perimeter fence, food parcels, escapees being fired upon and whatever else the confrères' imagination might conjure up. But all Redemptorists admired Esker, especially at a distance.

First Impressions

When Frank Tobin and myself and some others arrived at Athenry station we were met by Brother Enda, an institution in his own right, but as yet unknown to us. We helped each other load the pick-up truck with large strong trunks containing the prescribed requisites for the novitiate:

One new suit of black clothes.
Two extra pairs of trousers (one, at least, black).
One dark-coloured light overcoat (rainproof).
Six strong woollen shirts.
Four pair of woollen drawers.
Four woollen inside vests.
Three suits of pyjamas.
Three pairs of boots or shoes.
Ten pairs of black socks.
Six handkerchiefs.
Four collars and a black tie.
A black trilby hat.
Hair brush and comb.
Toothbrush and paste.
Shaving apparatus with a dozen blades.
Fountain pen.
Roman Missal.
Pocket money: – 40 or 50 shillings (about €3.)
Football boots and gymnasium shoes.
Bathing suit and Football-togs.

A large strong trunk.

At time of Profession a Chesterfield suit.

Ration book. [Then in the text but obsolete by my day]

Articles made entirely or partially of gold, silver, or silk are not allowed.

There was also a fee of £50, which amounted to perhaps 60-70% of college fees in the Juvenate at that time.

With all our worldly goods on board, we ourselves climbed on to the back of the truck for the final leg of our journey. It would be somewhat of an exaggeration to say that Brother Enda drove the four kilometres in almost as many hours, but speeding was not one of his habitual faults. I remember no more from that day apart from the fact that in Kiskeam that morning I had said a painful goodbye to my parents since I was 'going away for good'. It is not an easy concept to grasp today but that is how it was, and on those terms I left my father's house.

My next memory is walking around the eskers. An esker is a low sand and gravel hill left behind by the retreating ice age. Esker Riada, the most famous of them, is in fact a strung-out ridge of sand hills between Galway and Dublin and the historical dividing line between the two halves of the island, *Leath Chuin* and *Leath Modha*. Two fine eskers are within the grounds of the monastery and on that first full day in Esker the novice master, Fr Charlie McNiffe, walked us round and round like colts on the long reins. I was jaded.

Some three weeks after arrival in the novitiate we began a fifteen-day retreat but were allowed to speak once or twice a day. At the end we were formally accepted as novices. Up to that we were classified as postulants. Again, at the end of the novitiate, before making our profession as Redemptorists, we made another fifteen days retreat, this one in total silence.

'A Year To Break Them'

Even though the novitiate was approached with fear and trembling I found it a more congenial form of existence than the Juvenate. For one thing, there was more manual labour and that suited me. The spiritual formation was of its time – strong on discipline, weak on substance. There were lots of silly rules, probably designed to trip up the novice and test his reactions.

The Chapter

The weekly chapter on Friday revealed the weaknesses not only of the novices but of the system of formation as well. Chapters have been part of Religious Life from its origins in or about the 3rd century. They fulfilled the purpose of guarding religious discipline and offered an exercise in humility and mutual understanding. When the community assembled in chapter, members were given the opportunity of publicly confessing to infringements of the Rule and had a penance imposed by the abbot or superior. Probably to ensure that the exercise was genuine, an essential part of the chapter was the '*proclamatio*' or the accusation of one monk by another of observed infringements not mentioned. The person entrusted with this office both in the novitiate and in communities at large was know as the *Zelator*.

When it came to my own novitiate, each novice was expected to confess to twenty or thirty faults and, in an effort to build up an adequate portfolio for chapter, people were prone to draw on the ridiculous, for example, 'I accuse myself of not taking proper care of my toenails.' Another confrère, resorting to brevity, accused himself of 'having elbows on the table,' to which the novice master retorted 'Were they your own, brother?'

The next appointee to the office of novice master was Fr John McDonnell. At his first chapter, he endured hearing the long list of nonsensical accusations from one or other novice, then inquired if this was the general pattern, and on being assured that it was he issued an instruction that no novice was to accuse himself of more than three faults.

Moulding or Forming

The purpose of the novitiate as then structured seems to have been to get everybody into a particular mould. If novices were not prepared to conform to the contours of that mould they risked ejection. Our novice master succinctly articulated the philosophy of the novitiate when, referring to the novices, he said, 'I have only a year to break them.' He, too, had probably grown up on a farm and knew a thing or two about breaking horses. Breaking generous young men was more problematic.

Esker was a wild spot, not in its nightlife but environmentally. Every batch of novices contributed to the overall improvement of the place. One group built the swimming pool in the bog, another converted an open quarry-face into a beautiful Calvary, another planted a forest, yet another laid out the multiple walks around the eskers, and so on. This physical exercise was a Godsend for if these sturdy young men had undertaken a celibate life there was need for lots of physical exercise to keep the libido under control. By the time of our arrival in 1955, the Calvary had been completed and the swimming pool was proving a great asset to both novices and community. For the remainder of that wonderful summer we were allowed a swim most days, having first done our work assignment at the laying down of a tennis court, which in the event proved abortive. The swimming pool, too, eventually came to grief. Because intruders sometimes cut through the perimeter fence, the insurance company refused to give it cover and in the interest of safety it had to be demolished. Yet, the novices of former years who had sweated and slaved at the entirely manual undertaking of digging out the bog, mixing concrete and the like, can rejoice in the fact that the pool had served the community well for more than twenty years.

Daily Life
It was in the novitiate that we learned how to recite the Divine Office, the church's official prayer. Since it was pre Vatican II the office was in its older, longer and more complicated form. It was also in Latin. We learned lots of new terms and gradually began to feel at home in a clerical world, using terms such as *preces*, *antiphonarius*, *martyrology* without batting an eyelid. When reciting the Divine Office we normally sat for the recitation of the psalms and stood for hymns, but one of the hurdles our novice master had set up for us was that in the event of making a mistake in pronunciation or otherwise, we were to kneel for the remainder of the psalm. This meant that many of us spent a lot of the time on our knees.

We had charge of all the household chores, cleaning the toilets, scrubbing the floors once a week, dusting and sweeping and all that goes into keeping house. If the novice master saw anything less than perfect and made a reference to it we dropped on our knees at once. In fact we spent so long on our knees between praying and repenting that when, a few years later, a batch of my companions went to the Brazilian Consulate in England in order to get entry visas, there was a reluctance to grant them. Why? Because these young men were perceived to have a baffling disease of the knees. The first monk to go in was examined and the scales on his knees were spotted. He explained that the scales were from kneeling a lot. They didn't believe him. Then came number two, followed by numbers three and four. All had the same problem and the authorities were finally convinced of their *bona fides*.

Levamen

In the summer of 1956, about three quarters way through the novitiate, we had ten days 'levamen' (a kind of holiday) in Cluain Mhuire, our monastery in Galway city. The time here was highly structured but not as tightly as in Esker. The novice master led us to Ballyloughane, Renmore each day for a swim. It wasn't the most salubrious spot on earth, particularly when the raw sewage had been released. It was better not to study the water too closely or try to identify moving objects within it. We survived. Alleluia!

During the novitiate and later as students, we were allowed two visits a year from our relatives. Cornelius Cronin, better known as Con The Lord, was hired to bring my family because we did not have a car of our own. Con fulfilled part one of the undertaking by bringing my people to their destination and then proceed to visit his sister who was married a few miles from Galway city. There he loaded a cargo of poteen for distribution among his clientele in Kiskeam. So, all in all, each visit proved satisfactory to all concerned and in the spirit of St Alphonsus, nobody wasted a moment of time.

The Benefits

There is no doubt but that the novitiate introduced us into the life we could expect, both as Redemptorist students and later as priests and missioners. In the process of being moulded into the Religious Life as then understood, the personality took a battering and left a life-long negative mark on some, but the resilience of human nature enabled most of us recover and even blossom.

On the positive side, this moulding into community enabled us to put aside our differences and idiosyncrasies in the cause of the gospel. This is probably at the root of our strong tradition for being able to handle the big job, such undertakings as Regional Missions and Solemn Novenas. It also meant that issues such as personal needs and job-satisfaction were very low on the priority scale. In fact, they were not on it at all.

Those of us who suffered under – and came through – this old regime often joke about those days. But we are open-eyed about modern developments, too. The ideal is elusive.

CHAPTER FOUR

Cluain Mhuire (1956-1963)
A mediaeval town

Vertical Plant

The studendate, the monastery in which I was to spend the next seven years, stood on rising ground between Moneenageesha Cross and Mervue on the eastern edge of Galway city. It overlooked Loch a' tSáile just below and Galway Bay on the horizon. The house was large, the room and windows large, the air fresh and bracing. Cluain Mhuire was a good place both in summer and winter. It was more than that too. And it is the 'more' that fascinates me. Cluain Mhuire was in essence a mediaeval town, or in more prosaic terms, it was what the Americans call a *vertical plant*, raw material coming in one end and the finished product emerging at the other. In our situation, the raw material was the newly professed novice and the finished product was the ordained priest.

Cluain Mhuire was built in the late nineteen thirties. It replaced the seminary at Esker where our students had trained since we settled there at the beginning of the 20th century. In fact Esker had also been the studendate for Australian students, since we had responsibility for a fledgling mission in that country until it became an independent province in 1925. Building Cluain Mhuire was a bold venture undertaken by a large-minded provincial named Hugo Kerr. At the time, Hugo, a native of Belfast, was in his thirties. He saw the potential of an expanding Redemptorist Congregation in Ireland and the need for a healthy environment, good educational facilities, and access to a university. To that end he acquired thirty-six acres of good farmland sufficient to house the students and meet their basic food requirements.

As fortune would have it, the farm wasn't just any thirty-six acres. This one had the history of Ireland in its soil. On his 'wondrous winter march' to the fateful Battle of Kinsale in 1601, Hugh O'Donnell had camped at the bottom end where the

Dublin road separated it from Loch a' tSáile. The old coach road to Tuam used by Daniel O'Connell and many another patriot, ran north through our front yard; the only identifying marks in my time were a few trees that grew on either side of the old roadway immediately to the right of the Sacred Heart shrine. Finally, the entire farm had been part of the Joyce Estate, which came to be divided up on foot of the Land War and the changed administrative scene in Ireland.

The Community

In my time (1956-1963) the student body reached its zenith at one hundred. To that number was added the staff of brothers and professors, which brought the entire Redemptorist household to between one hundred and twenty and one hundred and thirty. Added to that number was a farm worker, Mr Willie Kelly from Connemrara, a quiet and easy-going man who lived in a house on the property. We often quoted another Connemaraman who knew Mr Kelly and summed him up well in his Galway accent, 'Willa Kella, vera steada fella.'

The community in Cluain Mhuire was young and energetic. The students were all in their late teens or early to middle twenties. The staff was on average about ten or fifteen years senior. The presence of a few older members of the province added a certain age balance to its overall composition. These older men, mostly retired from home and foreign missions, were easy to live with and acted as confessors and role models. The single focus of the house was study, a house of studies if ever there was such. It was not a university hostel. It was our home. It had an entire educational system all its own, running parallel to the university system but with approximately twice the number of study weeks per year.

Academic Year

Our academic year started on 16 August and ended on 27 June. During my time a break of a few days was conceded at Halloween. There were breaks also for Christmas and Easter. We made the five-day silent retreat during Holy Week and had a holiday atmosphere during the Easter Octave. The autumn term began with another five-day silent retreat prior to starting class on 16 August. During the rest of the year we had a day of retreat per month.

It must have been during one of these retreats that I took a decision to keep my temper in check. It was never very bad but I have what is colloquially called a short fuse and my efforts at keeping it in check have not always been successful. If I have a row with somebody, I like to think of it as being in the nature of a Celtic battle, intense and short-lived. I particularly detest getting embroiled in embarrassing dogfights apropos of nothing. Another resolution I remember making and keeping was to avoid punctuating conversation with the name of Jesus or current expletives. But if Liguori's men were to ask, 'What? Never!' Then, with Captain Corcoran in *HMS Pinafore*, I too, would have to humbly respond, 'Well, hardly ever!'

Classes were held every day except Thursday, which traditionally was a recreation day in honour of the events so strongly associated with it, the Lord's Supper, the Blessed Sacrament and the priesthood. Students were expected to get some study done on Thursdays but there was no compulsion. Sunday Liturgy was followed by the Mission Academy. At the academy we each took turns at preaching, using a ten minute extract from sermons composed by older missioners or well established 19th century preachers such as Fr Tom Bourke, the Dominican orator or Bishop Moriarty of Kerry. We preached in both English and Irish before an audience of fellow students and professors. Having delivered ourselves of the extract to the best of our ability we stood there on the rostrum while a public critique of elocution, delivery, gestures and overall effect was delivered by staff and students. The critique was generally kind, but some classmates, in order to have something to say if asked, would comment on what they knew to be our predominant weaknesses, e.g. pronouncing the 'th' or with Dubliners the use of 'q' sounds instead of a hard 'c' as in 'cow.' One could sleep through a midlander's sermon and still bluff one's way through a critique if asked. 'Th's were their downfall and week-in week-out they were put through their paces with 'Betty':

Betty bought a bit of butter.
The bit of butter Betty bought was bitter.
If Betty bought a bit of better butter
It would make her batter better.

Almost invariably this would come out as:

Behhy bough a bih of buhher
The bih of buhher Behhy bough was bihher
If Behhy bough a bih of behher buhher
It would make her bahher behher.

The preaching rota was such that in the course of any given year one might preach twice in English and once in Irish. This went on throughout the entire seven years.

Since running schools was not part of our apostolate, the number sent to university was limited. When those students finished their degree they resumed class with the rest but had to do an extra year in order to supply for church history and certain philosophy courses that were not covered at university. Meanwhile the Cluain Mhuire curriculum was followed in detail with examinations twice a year. However, since it was not an independent degree-granting college, and not accredited to any such, nobody got credit for their work. There was a sense that we didn't need such recognition. In these circumstances, if a confrère decided to leave the Redemptorists either before or after ordination he was left in a vulnerable position with nothing to show for all his years of study, and many a man with the equivalent of a doctorate or maybe two, had to begin as a first-year student at university.

The Curriculum

Our years of study were broadly divided as follows:

Rhetoric (1st year),
Philosophy (2nd & 3rd years),
Dogma (4th & 5th year)
Morals (6th & 7th year)

Rhetoric included English and Irish literature and logic. Philosophy studies were in metaphysics, ethics, psychology, epistemology, and cosmology. Side by side with philosophy went two years of church history. The next two years covered all aspects of systematic (dogmatic) and sacramental theology together with an equal amount of time given to scripture studies, both in Old and New Testament. Morals also included canon law and spiritual theology. All through the seven years there were ongoing studies in liturgy, church music, homiletics, singing and, of course, elocution. Because of our apostolate as itinerant preachers the latter was particularly significant for us Redemptorists. Three elocution classes a week were built into the curriculum together with an obligatory fifteen minutes private practice daily. Until the late 1960s most churches did not have an amplification system. We, therefore, had to fill the church with the unaided human voice. I often lament the passing of this art. It was highly technical and involved physical and psychological techniques concerning the nature of the building, the position of the missioner, the casting of the voice, the concept of one's audience.

Textbooks in philosophy and dogmatic and moral theology were in Latin and I was not a good Latin scholar. Consequently, it was not until after ordination and the end of formal examinations that I really began to grapple in a more personal way with these subjects. For our first year in the scripture programme we were fortunate in having an able and interesting professor named Fr Michael Baily from Ballymacelligot, Co Kerry. The richness of his learning and his capacity to communicate it was a gift to all who sat at his feet. Fr Frederick Jones, professor of church history, had a like enthusiasm for his subject and as history was a strong point with me, I delved into various aspects of it both on and off the curriculum. His field-outings, for which we prepared thoroughly, added considerably to our knowledge and understanding of the history of the church in our own land. My knowledge of history further expanded by attending occasional evening lectures at the university where I came into contact with the world of archaeology, first under the late Professor Duignan and later under Professor Etienne Rynne. The friendship with Etienne became a lifelong one and it was under his guidance that I participated in my only archaeological dig.

Personal Assessment
Although eternally grateful for the gift of reasonable health, long-term debilitating factors include atrial fibrillation, a weak back and intermittent migraine occasioned by hypertension. Academically, I never shone at examinations and was generally assessed as 'borderline' or more favourably, 'bright' but 'un-

even.' Illustrative of this latter was getting 85% in geometry and 0% in algebra in one exam and 97% in history and failure in French in another. At the end of primary education I had good Munster Irish due to the high standard at Kiskeam School. While my grandparents were bilingual they were dead before I was born. My parents were monolingual but used hundreds of Irish words in daily conversation. At second level school my facility in Irish suffered a set back from contact with Connacht parlance together with the revision of grammar and spelling in the 1950s and the introduction of the *cló Rómhánach*, the Roman script.

By nature I am left-handed but an intensive course in corporal punishment helped me adjust to the standard of the day. The negative side of that experience is that I cannot write very well with either hand. On the positive side, I felt the necessity of teaching myself the basics of typing while in Cluain Mhuire, an art perfected during the Pastoral Year after ordination. The acquisition of this skill opened up a new and liberating world. Whether the transfer from left to right hand has left its mark I cannot say for sure, but I can at times have slightly dyslectic tendencies (letters and sometimes words taking on a life of their own by jumping about or switching places).

About half way through the seminary days in Galway, a fellow student remarked that I had 'intelligent eyes'. The comment was music to my ears. I never forgot it for him because at that time I was finding it difficult to cope with Latin textbooks and some aspects of the curriculum. My real interests were history, archaeology, hagiography, forestry and horticulture and only one of these, history, was on the curriculum. I loved cattle too. Not that we did farm work in Cluain Mhuire, but watching them graze or lie in the fields always conveyed to me a sense of peace, of timelessness and wonder.

Gardening
Since games held little interest for me, it was in the garden, among the trees and the flowers that I found the opportunity for physical exercise and relaxation. Even after fifteen or twenty years of residency there was still a lot of heavy work to be done in terms of laying out of lawns and pathways together with the

planting and transplanting of saplings and trees. There was satisfaction in sowing seeds – antirrhinum, lobelia, alyssum and sweet pea in the greenhouse and a special delight in observing the tiny lobelia seed assert itself in breaking the surface of the soil. After that came all the tender loving care that is essential to successful horticulture. The paradox of gardening was my salvation in Cluain Mhuire. In the garden, time stood still, and in another sense it never went so fast.

Only Half the Story

All that I have recounted above is only half the story. Cluain Mhuire had a debating society, an English academy, an Irish academy, and a music academy. Each year the students produced three plays, two in English and one in Irish, together with a Gilbert and Sullivan opera. We had a thirty-piece orchestra and a six-piece jazz band called *The Sorrowful Six*. I myself wasn't in either play or opera but thanks to my background in Kiskeam Brass Band I played the trumpet in both orchestra and jazz band. In the course of the year we would stage several concerts and a *stunt* – a homemade farce with thinly disguised studendate characters, larded with topical 'digs' and references.

In the tight regime of Cluain Mhuire the stunt was a particularly important feature because it provided a mechanism for humorously airing student grievances concerning such matters as pressure of work, food, study, staff, anything. The stunt was, in a way, the highlight of the year's entertainment, except for those lampooned in it; and it must be said that these generally took it all in good part. There was fun in the stunt but not a sharp edge for the simple reason that in Cluain Mhuire there was no 'them and us'. Professors, domestic staff, students were all Redemptorists, living under the same rule, following the same timetable, living on the same corridors, sharing the same food and similarly affected by any restriction or alleviation that might occur.

The Orchestra

Harry Walsh, a brilliant musician from Cahir, Co Tipperary and two years my senior, conducted the orchestra in my time. Harry had ambitions for us. He even applied to Radio Éireann for an audition and it was agreed that the outside broadcasting unit would come to Cluain Mhuire and record a half-hour concert. Harry was excited beyond words. He had us practising at every possible opportunity, nice pieces, including material from the *Meister Singers*, *Tales from Hoffman* and arrangements of orchestral works by such classic composers as Mozart, Hayden and Beethoven.

It must be remembered that the student orchestra was always changing. Since the maximum number of years in the seminary was seven it could never be more than an orchestra of beginners despite the fact that some students were natural musicians and performers of high quality, including the conductor himself. Others had potential but needed more time to develop, and then there were people like myself, who would never make musicians but could make a contribution in the amateur circumstances. I certainly had the skill to produce good tone on the trumpet and get by with simple pieces, but my timing left something to be desired if I am to judge by Harry's gentle interventions concerning somebody in the brass line who wasn't sufficiently accurate on time. Those of us in the orchestra thoroughly enjoyed the experience but, at best, our playing left a lot to be desired, and by the time the outside broadcast van arrived Harry had us exhausted.

We played our pieces for the radioman and we played them again when he asked us. Then there was a long pause. We sat around waiting. Harry was at the proverbial 'high doh', wondering what the visitors thought of his orchestra. When nothing was forthcoming, he said to one of the technicians 'What do you think?' The reply totally deflated him but was the source of endless fun afterwards. In a strong Dublin accent the sarcastic technician turned to Harry and said, 'Did you ever hear someone emptying ashes out of a bucket?' The upshot of our dreams of an orchestral concert on Radio Éireann ended in playing for about thirty seconds in a 'round the country' programme on a Sunday afternoon.

Mediaeval Town
The studendate was like a mediaeval town in the sense that one could go for days, weeks or even months without ever stepping

outside the gate. Nor did the similarity stop there. We were largely self-sufficient, most of our needs being met from within. I never made a telephone-call in all those years nor have I any recollection of handling money, although it must have happened on the odd occasion.

Within the gates of Cluain Mhuire there operated a whole range of activities and services, both indoors and outdoors. There were games: Gaelic football, hurling, rugby, soccer, tennis, basketball, squash, handball and even an attempt at cricket on occasion. Indoors were facilities for snooker, billiards, table tennis and cards. For logistical reasons we were divided into work-groups called batches. Every student found himself on a batch for both an indoor and an outdoor assignment. The system was akin to mediaeval guilds. There were the printers, bookbinders, librarians, leather-workers, electricians, cobblers, builders, carpenters, stamp dealers and lemonade-makers. There were batches to care for the vegetable garden, the greenhouse, the orchard, the flower gardens, the hedges, the bees, the walks, the woodcutting that kept the furnace aflame. The Monastery had its own bakery, too, and batches operated in both serving at table and doing the wash-up.

Mervue Beauty, our prize cow, had the highest milk yield in all of Ireland in my first year. The little herd of cows kept up an all-year-round supply of milk while the farm also met our need for potatoes, turnips, cabbage, carrots and other vegetables. Grain was grown and the fresh straw used for packing mattresses. After the threshing in the autumn each student took his mattress to the farmyard, where he emptied out the old straw and filled the pallet with new. For a few nights afterwards the mattress would be humpy and bumpy but with a little bit of adjustment here and there it gradually took on the body contours and made for a good night's sleep.

The way in which one got into bed for the first few nights after getting new straw had a major effect on the long-term satisfaction of the mattress. If one got in the usual way there was a tendency for the mattress to sag in that direction, but if one carefully climbed in at the bottom and crawled up into a sleeping position there was every chance that in a few days time one had a delightfully comfortable niche in the middle. That accomplished, the occupant could resume his normal pattern of getting in and out of bed.

'Clifden'

Since we did not get home on holidays, there was need for a substantial break in summer in order to refresh the students. To meet this need we had a house near the head of Ardbear bay about two miles from Clifden in Connemara, where we spent close on six weeks. For that reason Clifden was a magic word. Mention of it conjured up excursions, lawn tennis, swimming, boating, islands, fishing, mountain climbing, reading, radio programmes and newspapers. Although more relaxed than the regime in Cluain Mhuire, the holiday in Clifden was tightly controlled by a multiplicity of rules of which a few, mostly those governing swimming and boating, were practical.

We were a novelty in the entire Clifden catchment area from Roundstone to Lettergesh and Leenane in those pre-tourist days. Necessary supplies were taken by lorry but the generations before us sent everything by train: boxes and tea chests and bags and linen and what not. The passage of this cargo through his station was a real headache for the stationmaster at Maam Cross because he had to itemise every single unit that went through on any given day. Not only that, in the evening all that information had to be dictated on the phone to Johnny Mahony, the stationmaster in Recess. Come late June each year, the station-master at Maam Cross would ring Johnny Mahony as usual, but on this occasion his opening greeting would always be the same: 'The hoorin' monks are back again!'

The summerhouse in Clifden was named Castellamare in memory of Thomas Falcoia, an influential adviser of St Alphonsus de Liguori and Bishop of Castellamare di Stabia on the bay of Naples. To draw any further parallels or comparisons between the Bay of Naples and Ardbear bay would require a greater imagination than mine. Lady Butler, one of the ubiquitous Ormond clan, previously owned the house. In the near vanished gardens one could still discern *the relics of aul dacency* in the terraced lawns and exotic but unkempt shrubs.

In Cluain Mhuire there were approximately fifteen bicycles for the use of students going to university. Students, not neces-

...ersity students, rode these to Clifden and there
... long list of applicants for the privilege of cycling
...e journey. The homeward trip was extended to sev-
... as students were more fit at the end of the holidays
...ded to take the longer and more scenic route by
Kyle...ore and Leenane, down the Maam Valley, on south to
Screeb and Pearse's Cottage and finally, home by the shores of
Galway Bay. Those not travelling by bike went and returned
from Clifden by a specially chartered bus. The journey was
made on or near 27 June, the feast of the Mother of Perpetual
Help.

There was much sleeping done during the first days in
Castellamare because the students were exhausted after the long
year and the exams that had just finished. Some light maintenance work was required in order to get Clifden into shape: cutting grass, trimming hedges, erecting the diving board, sinking
the boats. Our three boats were made of wood and after ten or
more months in a shed needed a few days under water to make
them seaworthy again.

We didn't enjoy the luxury of outboard motors or sails but
depended on the strength in our arms like most of our West of
Ireland contemporaries. By the grace of God we never had a
boating accident. We were not altogether ignorant of the ways of
the sea thanks to the tradition handed down from generation to
generation among the student body. Nevertheless, the inhabitants of the islands and coastal region were never fully at rest
until they saw us safe on *terra firma*. The most distant boating
excursion was the twelve miles to High Island, the site of a sixth
or seventh century monastic settlement. Only a special team of
stalwarts were allowed row that distance. Our normal destination for a full day's boating excursion was Inishturk, a journey
of six miles, three within the bay and three on the high seas.
Afternoon excursions stayed within the bay area but even there
the waters could be rough. I was more than happy to reach dry
land one stormy evening after all hands had been fully occupied
for a considerable time: one at the helm, six on the oars and one
or two with tin cans bailing out water as fast as they possibly
could in an effort to save us from beings swamped.

On reaching Inisturk we would light a fire and cook a dinner.

If we were fortunate enough to catch fish on the outward journey they were added to the menu; but we always had plenty of food – the potatoes boiled in seawater were particularly tasty. A memorable excursion for myself was the day we were followed by a school of sharks. It was not our boat that the sharks had in mind but a pair of porpoises that were leaping ahead of us in the hope of escaping with their lives. Our worry was that the sharks might capsize the boat if they came too near. It was a relief to land on the island that day. We stood on the shore watching them go by, the dorsal fins plainly visible and their snorting and snoring like the grunting of pigs. Another exciting memory, but without the anxiety, is that of an afternoon boating within Clifden bay when we ran into a shoal of mackerel. On pulling in my line I found a fish on each of the five hooks.

The holidays in Clifden might be described as robust: swimming, walking, mountain climbing, cycling, tennis. During the holidays in Clifden we thought nothing of walking eleven miles to Slyne Head, having a swim, eating our picnic lunch, resting for a while and walking the eleven miles home. Excursions to the Twelve Pins involved walking five or six miles, climbing anything from three to nine mountains and walking home again. The most I ever climbed in a day was seven and there were times when I found myself sitting on a ledge from which I felt I could neither ascend nor descend, and asking myself why I had set out at all.

There was a generous King family living among the mountains who looked forward to our coming like the arrival of the swallows. We spoke of their home as the buttermilk house because they always offered this refreshing drink to the young clerical mountaineers who were probably the only people to pass their door in the course of the year. In time, probably about 1962, the Kings bought a car but because of their remoteness, a garage had to be built for it some three or four kilometres from the house. Nevertheless, they were delighted with the purchase because they could now drive most of the long journeys to church and shop.

'The Beauty of this World'
Cycling excursions, of which we were entitled to two per sum-

mer, allowed for travel further afield. Of the various options available, Lettergesh was the most popular. There the loveliest Atlantic waters lapped an extensive deserted beach. Facing us was Boffin Island and at our back, the fifteen hundred foot Diamond Hill. After a swim and the excursion lunch it was customary to climb the Diamond. On the homeward journey by Moyard, weather permitting, the play of the declining sun on shore and hill created entrancing scenes. I can still feel the pain of it, the deep painful yearning that Patrick Pearse must have felt when he wrote,

The beauty of this world hath made me sad
This beauty that will pass.[1]

The Twelve Pins, too, plainly visible from Castellamare, were always enchanting. It was particularly wonder-full to sit and contemplate them change colours as if one were looking at a motion picture. I can appreciate the opinion that the Pins are impossible to paint. They just keep on changing, blue to purple, to vermilion, to rose and shades that I can neither remember nor name.

Clifden was not perfect. While it had a lot of attractions, I found it a lonely place at times. This loneliness had something to do with incompleteness, so much beauty and the absence of feminine company. Clifden also had at least two other serious drawbacks. The waters in the upper reaches of Ardbear bay did not differ greatly from the brown bog water of the Salt Lake that fed into it. This was unfortunate, particularly in a country where the most beautiful unpolluted ocean lapped the western seaboard from Kerry to Donegal. The other serious drawback was the weather. While not denying that we got fine days, and on the rarest occasions a fine summer, near interminable mists and rain kept coming in over Errislannan to deprive us of much needed sunshine. It was hope that kept us going, hope that tomorrow would be fine, and often, as the song says, 'tomorrow never came.' But in spite of the drawbacks, the holiday in Clifden was a welcome break from the study-year and it was with genuine enthusiasm that we looked forward each year to the return of 27 June.

---

1. Pearse, Patrick, 'Renunciation' in *The 1916 Poets*, p 24.

Sunshine or rain, 6 August and return to Cluain Mhuire came all too soon. Yet, there was something pleasing about being back in one's own private room, after sharing accommodation throughout the summer in a dormitory, a stable, an oats loft or a marquee. The hedges, lawns and gardens of Cluain Mhuire would have gone wild in our absence. We would set to work immediately and after two or three days of adjustment we were launched into a five-day silent retreat. We emerged from it to celebrate the Assumption and on the following day, 16 August, the new academic year began.

Ordination

Up to my second last year, our students were allowed to be ordained at the beginning of their final year of study. Ordination day was usually around 24 August. It was always a wonderful occasion not only for the *ordinandi* but also for the entire house. After all, it was the goal at the end of long years of intellectual, moral and spiritual formation. One month later, a batch of newly professed novices would arrive from Esker to begin the long haul, and to each was assigned a 'guardian angel' to introduce them to the ways of Cluain Mhuire.

Shortly before my own turn came for ordination the authorities in Rome issued a decree to the effect that ordinations could not take place until students had completed at least half of the final year's study. Because of this my ordination scheduled for August 1962 was deferred to 20 January of the following year. And as it happened, that winter was the worst since 1947. My uncle, Fr Thade Murphy flew in from Tasmania. My sisters Anne and Eileen left a New Zealand summer. It is obvious in the photographs that they were frozen but so were we all, though perhaps not as badly as they.

We were allowed three days vacation at home plus the days travelling. First there was the journey south through the snow and ice. We were often reduced to five miles an hour and it took the entire day. Returning to Munster and to Kiskeam was almost as novel as going to the novitiate in Esker seven and a half years previously. The neighbours rose to the occasion with bonfire and bunting. Mine was the first ordination from Knockavorheen. People came to the house almost round the clock. They came by car, tractor, walking, on horseback, by donkey and cart or trudging on foot over the snow and ice. At eighty years of age Bill Kenneally, father of my cousin and confrère, Fr Con, arrived on foot. He had tied *súgáns* and chains about his boots to keep from slipping and walked the four kilometres through the snow to pay his respects to the newly ordained. Over the three days many tears of joy were shed, many prayers of thanks were said, and after the seventy-two hectic hours it was back into class and the full routine of Cluain Mhuire. A house of studies indeed!

CHAPTER FIVE

Negotiating the Sixties
Mt St Alphonsus

The Pastoral Year

On 1 July 1963 the men ordained on 20 January were appointed to Mt St Alphonsus, Limerick to begin their *Pastoral Year*. This was a year of supervised ministry that involved sermon-writing, confessional practice, church work and, towards the end, our first parish mission. We were under the supervision of Fr Willie Murphy (Spiritual Director), Fr Seán Óg Connolly (Homiletics), and Fr Joe Corbett (Theological Mentor). It was a satisfying year, one of the best that I can remember.

Recognising that I was two metres in height and that no ordinary bed was long enough for comfort, one of Fr Willie's first comments was, 'Your bed is too short, Mr. Go down town and get it extended.' That I promptly did. Behind Willie's abruptness there was truly warm heart, something he generally concealed except in relation to the Legion of Mary. Legion envoys who travelled from Limerick to the ends of the earth for the sake of the gospel will testify to Willie's devoted attention to these young men and women who must have looked forward so much to his weekly individual letters with all the local news and evolving friendships and relationships among the legionaries in the city.

Willie's deep commitment to the Legion was a decided advantage to us in the Pastoral Year. He appointed us spiritual directors of various praesidia throughout the city. These appointments opened the way for contact with the outside world, something we had not experienced since going to the novitiate many years previously. Our charges were mostly junior praesidia with presidents chosen from the senior branch. We had a Legion meeting at least once a week and during one holiday period I had as many as seven. The office also involved attendance at other Legion functions, be they Commitium meetings or farewell parties for Legion envoys assigned to overseas work.

What I remember most of those days is the high quality and dedication of the young women who were presidents of the junior praesidia. They were good living, deeply committed and, true to Limerick girls' reputation, enchantingly beautiful. Within a few years I celebrated the wedding ceremonies of a number of them. And one reason why I myself didn't marry is that I'd have wanted them all.

Towards the end of the Pastoral Year, in May 1964, we got our appointments both long- and short-term. Some were sent to the Philippines, others to Brazil, and myself to Mayo. Naturally, after all the years of training and being psyched up for giving one's life to God on far foreign fields, two weeks in Crossmolina fell a bit short of the dream. But then, it is from what we call the home-missions that the Redemptorists in Ireland have earned their identity. Both in the hearts of the people and in the folk tradition, the Redemptorists are nothing if not the missioners.

Monastic Routine

We weren't long in Mt St Alphonsus before discovering that just as there was a tight regime in the formation stages, so too with the life of a missioner. There was a tradition, a style, a routine, and a way of being. At that time there was a community of between fifty and sixty in the monastery and those of us who were appointed to the home missions – Jimmie McLoughlin, Tom Reynolds and myself – were well down the seniority scale. As far as I can remember, I was number forty-nine. There wasn't enough employment to keep us all busy. The work – parish missions, retreats to priests, nuns, schools, lay associations and the like – generally went by seniority and when it came towards the end of the line the pickings were thin enough.

At home in the monastery, life was structured from morning till night: rise at 5.25, meditation at 6.00, first round of Masses at 6.30, second round at 7.00, half an hour thanksgiving afterwards and then breakfast. There were no concelebrated Masses in those days. There were altars everywhere – church, monastery, upstairs, downstairs – so that the priests might manage to celebrate individual Masses either at 6.30 or 7.00 o'clock, that is, unless they were marked for Mass on the high altar of the public church at a later hour.

The community gathered for Particular Examine prior to the midday meal. Half of the hour's recreation following the meal was spent walking in the garden in twos or threes and the other half in the community room chatting, playing cards, or reading the newspaper. An optional thirty minute siesta was followed by Evening Acts, consisting of half an hour's meditation followed by half an hour's spiritual reading, both of which exercises were made in the privacy of one's own room. Before supper, there was another half hour's meditation and after supper an hour's recreation of the same structure as that after the dinner. The Great Silence (in contrast to the Little Silence which ruled the afternoon) began with Night Prayer at 9.30. The Last Signal at 10.30 consisted of one stroke of the community bell at the sound of which all lights were to be out. Thereafter and until the morning call, the silence of the grave prevailed.

The Divine Office was said privately. It sounds strange today, but some early risers would have Compline finished before morning meditation while others were starting Lauds after night prayer. The concept of sanctifying the whole day had got lost along the way and it was a question of somehow, somewhere, 'getting in' the Office. To avoid a mortal sin of omission one had to have the office completed by midnight. Priests were frequently under pressure to meet this deadline and were known to have read their breviary by flash lamp or the headlights of a car in order to escape the terrible penalty. Legalists found some alternative ways of discovering 'midnight'. There was midnight according to Greenwich Mean Time, midnight according to daylight saving time, and midnight according to 'sun time'. Since the west of Ireland is approximately twenty-five minutes behind GMT, it was, therefore, possible in Galway to avoid mortal sin and the fires of hell if a person 'got in' the Office before 1.25 am !

Among the privately performed devotion enjoined by our rule of life was a daily fifteen-minute visit to the Blessed Sacrament, the making of the Way of the Cross and the recitation of the Rosary. In the matter of study a missioner was expected to keep abreast of the theological and moral issues of the day and engage in sermon preparation. On a regular basis, confrères were assigned specific tasks of preparing papers of a moral, ascetical or liturgical nature to be discussed and defended before the community.

Breakfast was taken in silence. There was reading at table during dinner and supper except on Thursdays or special occasions such as the arrival of a confrère from another house, particularly if he had recently returned from the foreign missions. Thursday was always a recreation day. This meant that some of the tight structures that governed the day were more relaxed and some of the spiritual exercises mentioned above were either suspended or privatised. Other than that the monastery was almost totally a place of silence.

The regularity of this monastic observance was in sharp contrast to the pattern of mission life. The former offered stability, the latter mobility and provisionality. It was my intention to continue gardening in Limerick as I had done in Galway so in the autumn of 1963, at the beginning of the Pastoral Year, I took a lot of geranium cuttings and shepherded them through the winter. The following spring saw them burgeoning and by early May several dozen were potted and almost ready for market. At that point I was sent on the Crossmolina mission. On my return the plants had wilted. It was good lesson. A missioner's life involved letting go of personal preferences and interests and after Crossmolina the first thing I let go of was a favourite recreation – gardening.

A Shift of Mentality

Later in that summer of 1964, John Hoffinger, an Austrian Jesuit, came to Dublin on one of the first post-Vatican II lecture tours that became a feature of the 1960s. We, the members of the Pastoral Year, had permission to attend. I got to only six of the nine lectures because it was my very first time in Dublin and my management of time and distances left a lot to be desired. Hoffinger's message was fresh and simple. He preached a God who is Love, God as Father, and in 1964 that was big news. I have no memory of the detail of any of his talks but John Hoffinger made a profound impression on me, thus precipitating a shift of thought from a pre- to the post-Vatican mentality.

The first effect of Hoffinger's liberating message on me was trivial in the extreme but it was significant. Up to that time we never went out without being in full clerical dress. Now in an act of exuberance and liberation, I dismounted my bike, leaned over O'Connell Bridge and solemnly sent my one and only well-worn black trilby hat ignominiously sailing down the Liffey. I never replaced it. With hindsight, it was not an ecologically friendly act, but such were the old days.

Some time after my dehatification I was browsing in Paddy Lysaght's second-hand bookshop in Limerick city. Two books caught my eye: *Power and Poverty in the Church*, by the French theologian Yves Congar, and *Nazareth Diary*, by Paul Gauthier. I bought them. These two books, together with my previous experience of hearing John Hoffinger, had a profound influence on me. Hoffinger was a devout and learned man with a refreshing, life-giving presentation of a post-Vatican II spirituality. Congar's *Power and Poverty in the Church* is a compelling study of the negative and positive influences of the two issues named in the title. Gautheir's book, on the other hand, recorded the inspiring reflections of a French priest working as a navvy in the Holy Land. The new vision that fired me brought its own hardships as well as its joys. Not everybody appreciated the new thinking.

Retreat House Work

In the autumn of that year, 1964 I was assigned to our retreat house in Limerick's North Circular Road. It was a temporary assignment to replace John P. O'Riordan while he and his cohorts did their 'second novitiate' in Esker Monastery, Athenry. The second novitiate was akin to the Pastoral Year except that it only lasted three months. It usually took place after confrères had spent their first five years as members of one or more of our various Redemptorist communities throughout the country. It gave an opportunity for some stocktaking and reflection of how adjustment to the general run of Redemptorist life was going.

John P's absence gave me a taste of retreat house life. The nature of the work did not allow for the rigid structure of the monastery. The week began with the making of a hundred beds on Monday morning. Then parishes had to be visited, priests and promoters of the retreat movement contacted, personnel appointed to do the advance preaching so necessary for getting parish groups organised. Going around to parishes meant a lot of driving and it was about that time that I got my first provisional licence and Fr Vincent Kavanagh, the 'accompanying driver' politely inquiring if I ever read road signs. Kavanagh was dynamic and not only succeeded in filling the retreat house to overflowing for the weekends – the overflow bringing welcome custom to some local Bed and Breakfasts.

Back in Mt St Alphonsus for Christmas, work continued to be sparse and intermittent. While on a mission in Thomastown with Fr Geoffrey O'Connell in 1965 the Mercy Sisters invited me to give them their three-day Christmas Retreat and that launched me on another branch of regular Redemptorist apostolate, nuns' retreats. Two months prior to that, on 5 October, Fr Tom Magnier and myself attended a most memorable concert in the Savoy where Wilhelm Kemp gave a stunning performance of Beethoven's *Emperor* Concerto. And on a mission in Kinsale the following year we had the privilege of listening to the young Virginia Kerr sing the Alleluia from Mozart's *Exsultate Jubilate*. If I may be permitted to mention another matter in the same breath as Kemp and Kerr, Mozart and Beethoven, it was on the same Kinsale mission that we first heard *Musheen Durkin* and *Surrounded by Water*.

The 'Funeral Priest'
One of the more frequent assignments for those of us who were not much employed was that of 'funeral priest'. It was not a role that we younger folk relished and it is mildly amusing to reflect back on it. In the society of those days, one of the indicators of an individual's or family's status in society was determined by the number of priests at a funeral. Apparently some if not all of the undertakers would ask a bereaved family how many priests they required for the funeral. If the number exceeded that of all available secular priests in the parish, (they had priority) the undertaker contacted the Religious Orders to make up the deficit. He'd try the Dominicans, the Jesuits, the Augustinians, the Franciscans and us Redemptorists in search of auxiliaries. As often as not, it was the same individuals from the different Orders who turned up to on these occasions.

The undertaker's car would arrive at Mt St Alphonsus to collect the priest. Before leaving the monastery, he'd be given half a crown by Brother Mark to tip the chauffeur. For myself, scarcely ever would I have an idea of the name of the dead person, and on occasion, didn't even know if the deceased was male or female. The funeral priest was expected to attend the Requiem Mass and accompany the cortège to the graveyard. Since at that time there was no concelebration, most priests read their daily Office during the Requiem. The walk to the graveyard was often made in the rain, and to add to the gloom, there was nearly always a priest present who never failed to throw some gratuitous insult or disparaging remark in my direction. This intrigued me. A bit of research revealed that he had a grudge against the Redemptorists because of some family matter, and the poor man had never adequately dealt with it in himself. At the end of the graveside service, the undertaker's car was at hand to bring us home and on arrival in the monastery yard we'd take the half crown from our otherwise empty pockets, give it to the driver and bid him farewell or perhaps more appropriately, *au revoir*.

Idle in the Gulag

Aside from the occasional mission, little more than a few weeks per year, unemployment stared us in the face. It was a truly painful time. One rector, Fr Gerry Carroll, went so far as to apologise for not sending me out on missions more often. He didn't want a revolt of senior men on his hands.

The regime in the monastery was strict. As stated above, the day was tightly scheduled from rising time at 5.25 in the morning until lights out at 10.30 pm. There were set times for prayer and meditation, for meals and recreation. Newspapers were available in the Common Room and, if I remember rightly, we were allowed to listen to the news on the radio during remission without having to get special permission. Besides, one might not leave the house or grounds without the rector's permission. What was left? Reading, sermon-writing, study, prayer. Well, I prayed. I read all sorts of works on new theology, on liturgy and spirituality, even to the point of trying to digest Hugo Rahner's *Greek Myths and Christian Mysteries*. I wrote sermons that I have never preached, instructions that I never gave. Anything was better than being idle.

A Visit from the Black Dog

Eventually the whole claustrophobic world with its rigid struct-ures, lack of stimulation and unemployment took its toll. I got depressed. Fortunately, as I've learned since, mine was a reac-tive depression, brought on by the situation in which I found myself, but in the early and middle sixties, depression, reactive or otherwise, was largely unknown, let alone understood or fashionable. Nobody knew what was wrong with me and I didn't know what was wrong with myself.

How long does winter last
The winter of a troubled heart?
No spring in sight,
Nor hope, nor joy,
But pain, depressing pain;
And oh, the loneliness![1]

I couldn't read. I couldn't study. My sleep pattern broke, never to recover. In the depths of winter, I would go down to the burial vaults under the high altar of our church at Mt St Alphonsus and wander among the dead. I envied those who died young. This one died at 15; lucky fellow! That one died at 26. How fortunate! And on it went. I had no energy. I'd cry easily. I was in an earthly hell.

The one consoling thought at the time was that what I was enduring was leading me on the path of holiness. And then I learned that it wasn't. A flawed concept of religious obedience had reigned for generations. I was under the impression that if I kept the rule and was passively obedient to superiors, I was on the way to heaven. It was an attractive theological package: neat, simple and, unfortunately, wrong. Personal responsibility had somehow got lost along the way.

The sustaining consolation about becoming holy in my curi-ous circumstances came to a sudden end when I consulted a learned, wise and holy confrère who pointed out that things were not as I had thought. He said that growth and develop-ment involved taking one's life in one's hands and positively re-sponding to the situations that presented themselves. In other words, if I didn't fine my present state life-giving, I had a re-

1. Ó Ríordáin, John J.

sponsibility to do something about it. That rattled me. I next consulted another wonderful confrère, my namesake, Seán O'Riordan. He agreed. Seán and I then explored a transfer to the Redemptorists in the U.S.A. only to discover that things were no better there, and possibly worse. That door was quietly shut. I considered leaving the Congregation, but then, I didn't want to do that. I wanted to remain a Redemptorist missioner.

Dear Lord,
You string me out upon a cross
Like sea wrack on a storm-beach
Or a ling drying upon a trellis.
My soul, sorrowful,
Heart and mind in chains.
And no parole in sight
Save an ancient prayer:
Lord Jesus Christ,
Son of God,
Have mercy on me,
A sinner.

O faithful One,
You died between earth and sky,
In your confusion and your pain,
With no ready answer from above,
No earthly solution save suffocation.
Or was it love that broke your Sacred Heart
As you descended into the darkness
Praying to your Father:
Into your hands I commend my spirit?[2]

Recovery
While the depression lasted I never thought of going to a doctor. I didn't know that my condition was in the illness category. As things turned out, however, I tumbled to the solution myself. In late September 1965 an older missioner who was scheduled to give a school retreat in St Ita's College, Tarbert, could not fulfil the assignment. The rector asked me to take his place, and although jaded tired – from doing nothing – I went. After three

2. Ó Ríordáin, John J.

days' hard work in Ms McKenna's Secondary School, I was returning to Limerick on the bus when, at Loughill, it suddenly struck me that I wasn't tired at all. This seemed strange, as I had started off jaded, worked hard and ended up full of energy. A similar situation arose when sent on a mission to Rearcross and Hollyford, Co Tipperary. It was the reverse of what one would expect: starting off drained, and ending up energised.

Consequent on these and further such experiences, I began to reflect on the relationship between my state of being and the conditions under which I had been living. It was only later during my psychology studies in Seattle in the mid 1970s, that the mystery finally unfolded. Consequent on unemployment and the confined nature of our life at the time, I was always tired and listless because an intense reactive anger was burning up every ounce of energy within me. Painful as this period of my life was, its legacy was a wonderful pastoral gift, namely, an insight into depression which only experience can provide. Ever since I have little trouble in appreciating that sense of meaninglessness, of worthlessness that so often accompany visits from the black dog.

The Freedom of the City
On discovering that unemployment was the source of my difficulties I approached the then provincial, Jackie White, and told him that I couldn't continue to live like this. He gave me a kind of 'telling off,' after which I proceeded to ask his permission to get myself a typewriter of my own, an innovative thing in those days, comparable nowadays to asking for a car for one's own exclusive use. Jackie was a man of action. He granted me permission for the typewriter and shortly afterwards appointed me sub-director of the Arch Confraternity of the Holy Family in Limerick. At that time the ten thousand-man confraternity was the largest in the world and the moral power and prestige of its director equalled if not exceeded that of the city's mayor. By contrast, the office of sub-director carried a zero rating. But for me, it was perhaps the most significant assignment of my life. In developmental terms it ranks beside the Hoffinger lectures and the books by Congar and Gauthier. It meant work, work unlimited and, for the most part, at my own discretion.

I was thirty years of age, and now, for the first time since joining the Redemptorists at the age of eighteen, I was free to leave the monastery and its precincts without the superior's permission. It was within my remit to conduct a pastoral visitation of confraternity men's homes, and that meant just about the entire city. Furthermore, the sub-director was entitled to occupy a confessional in the church on Saturday evenings, a coveted privilege. For the next two years I walked every street in town and made many lifelong friendships. And as my clerical hat had gone cruising down the Liffey, my reactive depression must have done the same 'on Shannon's boiling flood' because, like the hat, it disappeared without trace.

Confraternity and Credit Union

The Confraternity had five divisions. Monday, Tuesday and Wednesday nights were for the men. The boys' confraternity, that is, the primary school division had their weekly meeting at 6.00 o'clock on Friday evenings. And some time in the 1950s, in response to an evolving culture, the Thursday night division was established for young men. As sub-director, I had partial responsibility for the young men and full responsibility for over a thousand primary school boys. The average Friday evening attendance was between nine hundred and a thousand. To alert the boys and encourage them to attend their meeting, the sub-director had a busy schedule on Fridays. A good part of the day, the entire school hours, was taken up with visiting every classroom in every boys' school in town, with the exception of the pre-first communicants and the one or other Protestant School. At the six o'clock service there was singing, prayer, preaching and Benediction of the Most Blessed Sacrament. On most occasions, another confrère would be celebrant at the Benediction. Otherwise the service was a solo performance by the sub-director for his thousand bubbling youngsters. In winter, I'd be wearing my *zimmara* (a flowing black cloak) and moving to or from the pulpit a murmur of 'Dracula! Dracula!' could be distinctly heard.

During my term as sub-director of the men's Confraternity, the Credit Union Movement was beginning to expand rapidly, and by God's grace I had a hand in the process. Our Confraternity Credit Union was the largest in Ireland, and we were being asked for help and guidance in setting up other Unions in parishes across Limerick, Clare, Tipperary, and beyond. My role was in the vanguard. At all the Masses in any given parish, I'd do the advance preaching, holding forth on the idea of a credit union, addressing its philosophy, its practical uses and decided advantages. Having thus spread my canvas, I'd go on to give details of a public meeting (usually on the following Tuesday night), with a view to launching such an organisation locally. This was really innovative life-giving work in which I am truly happy to have participated.

A Russian Invasion

It was about this time, 1967 if I remember rightly, that a Russian ship docked at Limerick. It was a floating school with as many as fifty or more naval cadets on board. The cold war was still on and the idea of having Russians around at all was enough to make some people nervous. Word reached me that these young men were suffering from cabin fever and would love to get out for a game of football or some such activity if the captain permitted. Feeling like an international negotiator, I headed down to the docks, went to the Russian ship and asked if I could see the captain. When stepping aboard I had this slight irrational fear that if the Russians get their hands on me, I may never get out again. The captain was pleasant, asked me my business and agreed that his men were free to play a game of football against whatever team we could put up. A day and time were agreed. The venue would be our own football pitch, the Fathers' Field. There was some excitement in mustering a team but it was done.

At the appointed time I returned to the ship and led the party to the field. Mrs Corr in the South Circular Road watched the procession of spick and span 'communists' march two by two behind the tall Redemptorist in his religious habit and wheeling a bike at his side. The incongruity of it all caught her fancy and she regretted that her son, then a reporter and photographer for the *Limerick Leader* was not present to record this unique occasion. All went well until the visitors lost the match, and nothing would do them but to seek a return game. The Limerick boys, having defeated Russia, so to speak, were not anxious to push their luck with a replay. We eventually settled for a basketball match in our gym. And whether the Russians won or were allowed to win, we all lived happily ever after.

Teaching in the Tech

In the fall of 1968 I was reassigned from the confraternity to teach religion and sociology in the Limerick VEC, a post which I occupied for the next two years. My appointment coincided with the publication of Pope Paul VI's controversial encyclical letter *Humanae Vitae*. The change of job meant that I lost my Saturday evening confessional slot and people rashly concluded that I had been suspended for being 'soft on contraception'.

The teaching post involved the regular technical school together with the Electrical Engineering School, the Motor Engineering School and the Marine School – all in O'Connell Street and O'Connell Avenue. It included too, the 'one day' boys' school in Thomas Street and the 'one day' girls' in St Anne's in Sir Harry's Mall. These 'one day' institutions were part of a pilot scheme aimed at children who had left primary school early and were bound to attend on a specific day each week until the age of fifteen. In all, I had sixteen hours teaching per week and while unsure about how much education I imparted to the students, I certainly received a considerable amount myself.

Faith Crisis

1969 was significant for being the year when childhood faith with all its fundamentalist certainties deserted me. It happened suddenly while teaching a class in the School of Electrical Engineering in O'Connell St, Limerick. I had been talking about the Lord's Covenant with Abraham as told in the Book of Genesis. In the course of discussion a student inquired if God had actually spoken face-to-face with Abraham. I replied, 'Yes he had,' but scarcely were the words out of my mouth when I began to question what I had said. I remember standing there in front of the students as the bottom fell right out of that childhood faith which had thus far sustained me. The answer I had given had always been my belief, but now it did not necessarily make sense. If God spoke, did he stand in front of Abraham and speak in the local language? Or was the situation quite other than I had imagined – an internal conviction on the part of Abraham perhaps?

It was a shattering experience and for the next twenty years and more I lived a difficult life, emotionally a believer, practically a Christian, intellectually an agnostic. I don't have a high-powered intellect with a capacity for abstruse philosophy, but the existence of what the Canadian theologian, Bernard Lonergan, terms 'that which we call God,' has ever since reduced me to a deep and uncomfortable silence. Faith never came easy to me after 1969. To cope with this uncertainty I allowed myself to be carried on the faith of the believing community. In a non-rational way I learned to lean on the Communion of Saints, on Hebrews 'cloud of witnesses.'

The crisis forced me to image God in a new way, learn to live with mystery, pray more humbly, 'Lord I believe, help my unbelief,' or further down the scale, 'Lord, if you are there at all, I thank you and wish to love you and do your will.' It is comforting to know that there's a bit of the atheist in all of us, and the fact that we have doubts is, in a sense, a sign that we also have at least some faith in what we doubt. There have been times when I envied the strong faith of some wonderful people, and yet, I am aware that there are others who are more at home with my own muddled struggle.

I can identify with McGuire's 'All or nothing' stance in Patrick Kavanagh's *Great Hunger*:

Health and wealth and love he too dreamed of in May
As he sat on the railway slope and watched the children of
    the place
Picking up a primrose here and a daisy there –
They were picking up life's truth singly, but he
dreamt of the Absolute envased bouquet –
All or nothing.[3]

I want to get God into my head, and in that attempt greater skulls than mine have cracked. Ever since that shattering experience in class, easy comfort in my faith has deserted me. I plough my furrow in the hope that all will come right in what we call 'God's own good time'. And I have a feeling that it will. That is

3. Kavanagh, Patrick, 'The Great Hunger' in *The Complete Poems*, p 88.

my 'joyful hope.' I continue to pray the old Irish hymn of Máel Ísu Ua Brolcháin,

Deus meus, adiuva me.
Tabhar dom do shearc, a Mhic Dhil Dé.
Tabhar dom do shearc, a Mhic Dhil Dé.
Deus meus, adiuva me.

Domine, da quod peto a te.
M'anam beidh lán ded' grá, a Dhé.
M'anam beidh lán ded' grá, a Dhé.
Domine, da quod peto a te.

My God, help me.
Give me your love, dear Son of God.
Give me your love, dear Son of God.
My God help me.

Lord give me what I ask of you.
O God fill my soul with your love.
O God fill my soul with your love.
Lord give me what I ask of you.[4]

Among the many contradictions in me is the fact that while struggling with an agnostic streak in myself, my favourite name for Christ is 'Jesus the Revelation of God'. Not only that, he is the focus of my life. I see or try to see all that is through his eyes. It is only when it comes to concepts of that which we call God, of mysteries such as 'in the beginning,' and 'life without end' that problems arise.

So ended the 1960s – a decade of change so radical that we are still coming to terms with its implications in both civil and religious life.

---

4. See: George Sigerson's translation in *Bards of the Gael and Gall*, pp 207/8.

CHAPTER SIX

Liguori's Men (1964-1969)
The Mission Tradition

Deeply Rooted

The mission tradition in which we Redemptorists were ordained is deeply rooted in Christian history. In one sense it goes back to the preaching of Jesus and his disciples and to the itinerant preachers of the early church. But in terms of an established method of renewal and revival of faith, it dates roughly from the days of St Norbert (1082-1134) and his reformed Canons Regular of St Augustine in the early 12th century. They were free to work over wide areas unimpeded by diocesan boundaries. Their missions were generally no more than a one-day stand and they addressed lengthy sermons on topics such as death, judgement, heaven, hell, eternity, frequentation of the sacraments, reconciliation of enemies, duties of landowners and duties of the married.

From the 13th century onward the mission tradition got enormous impetus from the emergence of the Mendicant Friars, especially the Franciscans and Dominicans. By the early 15th century, especially under the influence of splendid preachers such as St Vincent Ferrer and St Bernardine of Sienna the mission had evolved further. The day began with Solemn Sung Mass. The missioners would usually establish themselves on suitably raised platforms and preach for hours. From these vantage points they denounced the vanity of the world, the vices of the people, the degradation of the clergy, the troubles of the church, and they interpreted wars and pestilence of all sorts as the wrath of God coming down upon his sinful people.

After this loosening up process, so to speak, the missioners went on to topics such as repentance, the ending of feuds, the education of the local clergy, and the establishment of confraternities and societies for the support of the faithful in living the Christian life. They encouraged popular devotion, especially to the person of Jesus as Saviour and to Mary as Mother of God and our mother. In Ireland, as elsewhere on Continental Europe there are relics of those days and venues in the form of the Market Square Cross that has survived as a feature of some towns and cities.

Counter Reformation Missions

In the 16th century the church was convulsed by the Protestant Reformation. The Catholic Church's reaction to this upheaval is called the Counter Reformation. The Council of Trent (1545-1563) set about establishing the priorities and boundaries of Catholic life, and the parish mission played no small part in bringing the message to the people. The missioners' primary concern was preaching the core of the faith. The message was further reinforced and strengthened by establishing Confraternities of Christian Doctrine.

Key figures in the development of parish missions from the 16th century onward include St Ignatius Loyola, St Vincent de Paul, St Leonard of Port Maurice and St Alphonsus de Liguori. The 17th century saw a fuller development of missions and the growth of missionary Congregations and Societies of priests devoted to this work. It was my good fortune to come in at the end of the Counter Reformation era and experience some of that life before it passed away.

Naples to Limerick

Working as a missioner has given me the opportunity of studying my own tradition more closely. When I joined the Redemptorists in the 1950s the Order had a reputation for being tough. It was. We bore the stamp of the Counter Reformation: highly disciplined, mobile, evangelical preachers of the Word of God. Alphonsus Maria de Liguori founded our Congregation near Naples in 1732. He was a conscientious and able lawyer who abandoned the corrupt law courts of his native city in favour of dedicating his life to the service of the poor and most abandoned. To find them he hadn't far to travel. His native city of Naples had a glut of priests but the inhabitants of the country districts round about were utterly neglected.

From Naples the Congregation spread, first to Austria and Poland, later to Belgium, the Netherlands, England, Ireland, and over more than sixty countries of the world. The burial vaults beneath the high altars of our churches in Limerick and Dundalk reflect some of that story as the patronymics *Mac* and *O* are side by side with *von* and *van*.

At the invitation of William Monsell of Tervoe, later Lord Emly, Fr Frederick de Held, son of the Chancellor of the old Austrian Empire, and provincial of the then Belgian province, came in person to Limerick. Dr Ryan, the local bishop, was anxious to have a Redemptorist presence in his diocese and with a view to making a foundation there, a mission was conducted in St John's Cathedral from 19 October to 2 November 1851. The success of the mission is legendary and negotiations for a foundation were initiated. Meanwhile, more missions were booked for the following year in Derry, Enniskillen, Letterkenny, Westland Row in Dublin and St Michael's in Limerick. The Limerick foundation was formally inaugurated on 25 November 1853.

From their rented accommodation in Bank Place, Limerick, the community conducted their mission work. The Good Shepherd nuns supplied much of what was needed to make the chapel in Bank Place suitable for worship. John McCafferty, a Derryman, saw to the material needs of any Redemptorists giving missions in Ireland and did likewise for the new Limerick community. Brother James Patrick Walsh of the Limerick Christian Brothers in Sexton St not only taught English to the missioners but also provided them with accommodation, suggested the site for the new monastery and at a time of critical assessment was primarily responsible for persuading them to stay in Ireland. The foundation of our monastery at Mt St Alphonsus was laid in 1858 and the church was dedicated on 7 December 1862.

Expansion and Growth

The 1851 mission team was comprised of able young men from widely varying backgrounds: Joseph Prost (Austria), Vladimir Petscherine (Russia), John Van Antwerpen (Netherlands), Leo Van der Stichele (Belgium), and finally, a Scotsman named Edward Douglas, a member of the Queensberry family – yes, those! The missioners didn't spare themselves and within a few years had worked in virtually all major centres of population in the country. After a mission in the pro-cathedral, Dublin, Archbishop Cullen, later Cardinal, wrote to the rector of Mt St Alphonsus, 'The church was crowded at every hour from five o'clock in the morning to eleven at night.' Recurring issues needing attention on these missions included adult confirmations, rectification of marriages, and the reconciliation of those who had gone over to one or other of the many evangelical proselytising groups.

Retreats to Clergy and Religious

The missioners were sought for retreats to Religious and to diocesan priests. In the year 1867 alone, Redemptorists conducted retreats for the priests of the dioceses of Dublin, Armagh, Galway, Killaloe, Limerick, Ossory, Cloyne, Ardagh, Clogher, Dromore and Kilmore. Vocations to the Redemptorists multiplied rapidly and several Maynooth students transferred to the Congregation. In fact the first Provincial Superior of an independent Irish Province in 1898 was Andrew Boylan who had been bursar in Maynooth College and later Bishop of Kilmore. When he was bursar a rumour was circulating to the effect that he might be appointed to Kilmore. On foot of this a witty student who felt the need for an increase of protein in the Maynooth diet displayed a poster which read, 'Boil on! Kill more!'

My First Mission

In May 1964, towards the end of the Pastoral Year I was sent on my first mission. Four of us were dispatched to Crossmolina, Co Mayo. At that time we were still in the shadow of the Counter Reformation. The Second Vatican Council was in progress but its message had not yet percolated through either to Crossmolina or to the missioners working there. Nor was that mission different from others that followed for the next several years. The evening sermons and morning instructions were standard: Salvation, Death, Judgement, Hell, Eternity, Scandal, and Delay of Conversion. Then came a blistering sermon on 'The Occasions of Sin' and after that it was into the calmer waters of the Christian life: devotion to the Most Blessed Sacrament, the Passion of Christ, the Mass, Prayer, Mary the Mother of God, and Heaven. In Crossmolina I was assigned some of the 'safer topics': Confession, Our Lady and the Amende, that is, a sermon on reparation to Jesus in the Most Blessed Sacrament. I can't remember who preached on the Occasions of Sin but according to the folk tradition the congregation expected it on the Wednesday night.

'The Occasions'

The sermon on the Occasions of Sin was intended to address all sins. In practice, however, after some general remarks it focused on perceived or actual sexual misbehaviour. The sermon addressed the nature of the occasions, the obligation to avoid them, and the excuses of those who remain in the occasions. Then followed examples of persons, places, things, which one knows from past experience to be occasions that are likely to lead one into mortal sin. It may be a pub, a magazine, a person, a conversation, a bad book: 'A bad book is, in the hands of the devil, one of the most powerful means of destroying souls.' Of all the 'occasions' mentioned, it was lonely company-keeping that caught the popular imagination, and indeed, the imagination of the missioner also:

> I must still speak to you of one which is the most dangerous of all. I wish I could remain silent about it; but I am grieved, yes, sorrow-stricken, when I think of the souls that are murdered, and become a prey to Satan, by it. I cannot be silent; I must do my duty; I refer to that abominable practice of lonely company-keeping. This detestable practice of lonely company-keeping which, in recent years, has become so common is the real danger for our country.

This sermon dates from the early 1940s when World War II was raging and the country was in danger both from Churchill and from Hitler. From this paragraph, however, it is evident that the missioner had another view on the danger of the day.

Before opening his mouth on the topic of lonely company-keeping the congregation was fully aware of the missioner's stance – he was *agin' it*. Nevertheless, they relished his dramatic presentation together with his use of terms that might later come in handy in the confessional.

A New Phenomenon

What is not widely known is that in the late 19th century the entire issue of company-keeping addressed in sermons was a new social phenomenon. During the Industrial Revolution young men and women began to leave home in search of work in the new industrial centres. They didn't have parents at hand to arrange marriages for them, therefore with a view to arranging their own they began to 'walk out together' as the expression had it. It was the finding of an appropriate pastoral response to this new phenomenon that was exercising the minds of moral theologians and missioners alike – something like we are attempting to do today in terms of genetic engineering and nuclear war.

Up to the mid-nineteenth century, marriages were mostly hard-headed business deals transacted especially among the propertied classes. Individuals, and particularly women, had very little say in the arrangements. Church laws that may now seem oppressive, controlling or meaningless were introduced in order to protect the freedom of women in contracting such marriages. A couple rarely met before the wedding and if they did it was in the presence of interested parties, notably the families concerned. St Alphonsus, who was considered overly lenient, allowed couples to meet once or twice provided it was in the company of their families. Stricter theologians did not allow such laxity. Various theories were put forward in relation to courting: ban it altogether; allow couples to meet occasionally but not alone; recruit a chaperone or *gooseberry*, a role played by Barry Fitzgerald in the film, *The Quiet Man*. In all these circumstances strict rules were laid down for avoiding the occasions of sin.

Though the rules applied to all sin they became particularly identified with sins of a sexual nature. These occasions were categorised as remote and proximate occasions, with a further subdivision into involuntary and voluntary proximate occasions (VPO). When on a mission in Co Kilkenny some forty years ago, I got a copy of *The VPO*, a composition by three Walshe girls (popularly known as *Faith, Hope* and *Charity*) who had a capacity and a zest for fun and verse. In this composition, they considered the effects of the advice given to the men of the parish by our own Fr Jim Collier:

Oh! girls of Kilkenny, our day is nearly done,
For a dreadful thing has happened since the men's retreat
begun.
The boys have got instructions – 'keep your souls as white as
snow,
And avoid like any pestilence, the VPO.'

That's very good advice, you'll say, to render to the men,
But I tell you that you won't be very optimistic when
I impart this information, in case you mightn't know
That we women, just imagine! are the VPO.

And we thinkin' we were lovely, and that all the men should
be
Highly honoured if we looked at them condescendingly;
But now they'll have the notions, for no matter where we go,
Jim Collier says we're nothing but a VPO.

So we needn't dress up smartly in the fashions of the day,
For the boys won't give the glad eye – they'll look the other
way
If your skirt's abbreviated, or an inch your knee below,
It's all the same, you're branded as a VPO.

And what about the boys and girls who go out holdin' hands,
They'll have to give each other up – CSSR commands!
Sure every little Juliet will lose her Romeo
Jim Collier says, 'Beware me boys, the VPO!'

So I've come to the conclusion that there really is no use,
In edging up to fellows, for we'll only get abuse,
And though we're quite well able to cook and bake and sew,
The boys, O Lord! They wouldn't touch a VPO.

Now it's really very serious for the girls, don't you see?
And we'll never get a husband and I think we'll have to be
Quite content with old maidism and you may be sure we'll
grow,
Into V-ery P-retty O-ornaments, but not a VPO.

Confessions
Celebrating the Sacrament of Reconciliation (Confession) was

considered an integral part of making a good mission and seen by the missioner as one of the chief yardsticks of success or failure. It was gruelling work for the missioner who spent up to nine hours a day in a stuffy and cramped confessional. The enthusiasm of the people for confession can hardly be imagined today. Even in the depths of winter people would walk barefooted for miles. They would wait in line for hours and even days. During the 1911 Redemptorist Mission in Kiskeam my mother remembered bringing buckets of tea to the church in the middle of the night for the waiting crowd. Youngsters were often engaged to hold places in the queue while penitents availed of temporary respites.

Blaming the French
Confession in the 19th century wasn't a matter of popping into the confessional for a minute or two. The standard practice for hearing confessions was two to the hour. In the confessional both priest and penitent were expected to explore failures under the headings of the Seven Deadly Sins, the Ten Commandments, the Six Precepts of the Church, the Four Cardinal Virtues and more. Fr Petscherine was reported to Rome for hearing confessions too fast: he was hearing three to the hour. Rome sent him a stern reprimand.

Some missioners short-circuited the system. On a mission in Youghal in the 1970s, a delightful elderly woman told me laughingly of her youthful encounter with the above mentioned Fr Jim Collier in the confessional. The missioner pulled back the slide and before the girl got time to bless herself he inquired. 'Do you keep company?' 'I do,' said she. 'Are you prepared to give up the young man?' said he. 'No,' replied the spirited young damsel. And with that the slide closed as swiftly as it had opened.

The detailed style of confessing came from an unfortunate mediaeval analogy. With the rise of legalism in the 13th century the 'confessing' aspect of celebrating the sacrament was put on a par with giving evidence in a civil court. Added to that was the Jansenistic influence of the French church. Cornelius Jansen, the 16th century Flemish bishop whose name is forever linked with this narrowness, lived and died without knowing what trouble his writings would cause across Europe and the world. Jansen saw limits to the mercy of God and the Salvation wrought by Christ Jesus. The Grace of God did not appear to him as the free gift that it is. Alphonsus de Liguori had several theological tussles with the Jansenists. His writings were publicly burned in Maynooth College, and that despite the fact that his writings have earned him the titles Doctor of the Church and Patron of Moral Theologians.

Priests have at times been criticised for asking too many questions in the confessional, for 'being nosey in the box'. No doubt some of them are. What is not generally known is that priests were bound under pain of mortal sin to comply with the guidelines laid down by theologians, some of whom had rarely if ever heard confessions. For a man with any tendency towards scrupulosity, then, the confessional was little short of a torture chamber.

It was in Borris-in-Ossory, Co Laois that I had one of the nicest experiences associated with hearing confessions. It hadn't anything to do with reconciling the Playboy of the Western World or transforming the village atheist into another St Paul. Like many of the lovely things in life it was overwhelming in its simplicity. I had been hearing confessions for a considerable time after morning Mass on a cold day. The priest's compartment had a half-door and a curtain. And through that curtain a woman pushed a bowl of hot soup. May the Lord, who doesn't allow a cup of cold water go without reward, fulfil her heart's desire.

The Mystique of the Missioner

The missioner enjoyed an exalted status in the community. He was seen as larger than life, asexual, and otherworldly. Few knew where he lived or came from. He was in the church but, in a sense, not of it. He belonged neither to parish nor diocese and in consequence had a freedom of speech rarely enjoyed by others. He introduced singing, Benediction and the use of incense for the first time into many Irish churches. And what was altogether confusing for both clergy and laity in the 19th century, he didn't drink punch. It is not that the missioners did not take alcoholic drink, but being Continentals, they had no tradition for strong drink while an occasional glass of wine was welcome. It was the abstention from punch that first earned the Redemptorist missioners the sobriquet *Holy Fathers*.

The refusal to drink punch was a delicate matter because it impinged on the realm of hospitality. It came to a head when the fathers declined a welcoming drink of punch proffered by Dr Patrick MacGettigan, Bishop of Raphoe. He felt that his hospitality had been spurned and relationships remained strained during the mission. To add fuel to fire during the evening mission service the preacher said something that infuriated the bishop. Fr Prost, the superior, realised that the situation called for urgent corrective action. Directly after the mission service he followed MacGettigan into his house and said, 'My Lord, I am exhausted, and would greatly appreciate a glass of punch.' Thereafter, a mission rarely ran more smoothly.

The Great Sermon and Morning Instruction

The 1941 *Blue Book* – still in use in my young days – comprised a series of sermons and instructions that experienced preachers had assembled. These were recommended for use either verbatim or as models for one's own compositions. Every missioner would like to believe himself to be a fine preacher. The dogs in the street may know that he isn't, but it would be the ultimate affront to suggest to him that he was anything less than a reincarnation of Bourdaloue. On that subject the phlegmatic and witty Fr Geoffrey O'Connell once remarked that you could tell a missioner that he had lost the faith or that he was grossly immoral, but you daren't say that he could not be heard in church or that he wasn't a good preacher.

In terms of prestige, the preacher of the evening mission sermon, or Great Sermon, was top cat. Morning instructions belonged to a different genre and might be handled by lesser mortals. The morning instructions were catechetical: the Commandments, Grace, Sins of the Tongue, The Trials of Life, Sanctification of the Day, The Holy Souls. The Great Sermon on the other hand dealt with such topics as Salvation, Death, Judgement, Hell, and of course 'The Occasions'. These sermons were passionate appeals to the mind and heart, to the emotions and the will, especially the will to change, the will to be converted to the Lord.

Accommodation and Maintenance

A seasoned missioner's stock in trade wasn't confined to sermons and instruction. He possessed a whole range of survival techniques connected with accommodation and maintenance. Cold unused rooms carried danger of damp, unaired beds. For that reason, on the night of arrival in the parish some missioners only partially undressed when going to bed. They might also conduct a dampness test by placing a pocket watch (or a mirror) between the sheets to see if it misted over. Pleurisy or pneumonia was a real hazard. Some missioners learned this the hard way while more than one found an early grave. Prior to the advent of the public address system even a cough or a cold would play the puck with one's preaching voice.

When the preacher of the Great Sermon came down from the pulpit he was usually in a lather of sweat and wrapped himself in a zimmara, a full-length black woollen cloak that was also a godsend during long hours in a cold confessional. In my own mission career I have experienced many of the above features. I have also experience the wonderful improvements and if the modern missioner has a sleepless night it is unlikely to be caused by the cold.

Strange Things

There was another concern about accommodation that no parish priest could meet. From time to time I experience what the Scots call strange things. Things that go bump in the night are not all products of a fertile imagination. On and off missions I have frequently experienced 'the three knocks'; seen ghostly forms in the night; felt or heard invisible presences, and the like. On a humorous note, I had one of these para-normal experiences in a parochial house, now happily demolished. Next morning during breakfast the non-resident housekeeper in her pronounced Cork accent said, 'Sometimes the curate is afraid to stay here on his own because the house is *haaaunted*.' I don't blame him at all.

I mention these things because there are people for whom such experiences are outside their range of perception. Nevertheless, psychologist William James points out, (and I rely on the late John Moriarty for the quote), 'there must be no premature closing... on reality.' Moriarty goes on to say that,

Most of us do close our account with reality and say that reality is such and such. That's what it is and no more. So we have closed our account the way you close your account with the bank. You have no more transactions with the bank or whatever it is. There's a heaven up there, there's a hell down here, and in the middle there's the earth, and this is the place where you're damned or saved. Now to have that and only that vision of the universe is, it seems to me, to have closed your account with reality.[1]

When I encounter strange things or am dogged by agnostic leanings, I keep my reality account open.

A Clerical Dinner

If Counter Reformation theology survived well into the 1960s, so did the clerical dinner. Such meals were part of a long-standing tradition and took place on special occasions, one such being the parish mission. As well as having us missioners, then, the parish priest would also invite some clerical friends to dinner. The meal itself was served in the mid-afternoon. It was a solemn affair at which the parish priest's reputation for hospitality was at stake as was his skill at carving a joint.

There was more than food involved. The clerical dinner was an occasion for social bonding and it lasted for hours. The resident housekeeper drew on other housekeeper friends to help in the kitchen and generally nothing was spared. After the meal we would adjourn to another room so that the housekeepers might tidy up. My memory of the adjoining room is one of cards, cigars, whiskey punch and clerical gossip. The more thoughtful senior missioners would make an excuse for me to leave the company, knowing that I might need to look over the text of the Great Sermon because in those days we did not take sermon notes into the pulpit.

1. From John Moriarty's lecture on 'The Exodus Theme And Personal Development' at the School of Personal Development, Cluain Mhuire, Galway, July, 1987

The Mission Stall

No mission would be complete without the presence of one or several mission stalls run by independent traders and stocked with religious goods – rosaries, crucifixes, medals and a variety of holy pictures including the Sacred Heart, the Mother of Perpetual Help and St Anthony. For the duration of the mission the stalls would be located along the roadside or sometimes within the church grounds. For youngsters the stall was the highlight of the mission. It had a kind of Santa Claus status. The interior of the little canvas-covered shack glittered under the glow of candlelight. The candles in time yielded to oil lamps, aladdins, tillys, gas and electric. However, with the brightening of the stall lighting the enthusiasm of the children wasn't dimmed a whit. One excited youngster said it all when he asked my confrère, 'Father, will there be a *tint*?'

In their hey-day, some of these traders played not only a colourful but a significant role in the mission. They were quasi-confessors to the local people. Like the missioners themselves they were strangers. They were around all day and people waiting for confession tended to confide in them. The traders offered words of comfort and were often able to advise on the choice of confessor. Like the journeymen and the missioners themselves, the stallholders are still there but gradually disappearing. Transport, accommodation, loss of interest in their products and their own children finding alternative ways of living, have all contribute to their demise.

The Close of the Mission and the End of a Cycle

The final Sunday night saw the solemn close of the mission during which both missioner and parish priest expressed all appropriate thanks. On the following morning there was a special Mass for the dead, after which the missioners were taken to catch a train or bus home to the monastery or directly to another mission. People were lonely at our departure while the parish priest relaxed with the satisfaction of a farmer seeing the threshing machine leave his haggard in autumn. This is the day when, according to the story, the parish priest having seen off the missioners, turns to the housekeeper and remarks, 'They're gone now and there isn't a pound or a mortal sin left in the parish.'

At the beginning of my mission career the cracks were already appearing in the old system. Urban attendance at the annual retreat was beginning to show a slight decline. Missioners and parishioners were feeling that something more than the 1941 *Blue Book* was required to hold and nourish a congregation. If the old themes of Death, Judgement, Eternity, Heaven and Hell were to be effective they would need an entirely new language to communicate any sense of the mystery involved. A number of efforts were made in the mid-sixties to meet the needs that were becoming more obvious with each passing year. And then, at the end of the decade several factors coalesced so that out of the smouldering embers of the Counter Reformation Mission, a fresh spark set us aflame. We called it *The New Mission*.

CHAPTER SEVEN

The New Mission (1970-1980s)
A daring and exciting venture

Winds of Change

In the early winter of 1969 we Irish Redemptorists elected Fr James McGrath as our provincial superior. He was large minded, big-hearted and energetic, with a lot of experience and wisdom gleaned from eight or nine years of mission work in Latin America. Jim immediately set about putting the province on a sound theological and financial footing. A six week fundraising campaign necessitated the laying aside of old monastic structures in favour of a more modern form of religious life. The fundraising techniques taught us by Mario Martinez having achieved their purpose were quickly adapted and applied with equal success to mission planning; for example, not doing any serious business over the phone and not going alone when arranging a mission.

The swift revitalisation of theological thought was due in part to missionaries returning from Brazil, India, and particularly the Philippines, where the vice-provincial, Fr Steve Mahony had long been encouraging the study of Vatican II theology. There was the inestimable contribution of Fr Seán O'Riordan, then attached to our Alphonsian Academy in Rome. His visits home, his lectures, courses, conversation and charming personality brought us into a new and exciting way of understanding church and religious life.

And finally, since the early winter of 1969 we were blessed in an administration where the right people in the right places allowed space for the talents of each individual to blossom. McGrath, the provincial, being a man of vision, was open to new initiatives that offered potential and Fr Stan Mellett, the new rector of Mt St Alphonsus, was of like mind. The structure was set for development and it wasn't long in coming.

A Vital Spark

What became known as the *New Mission* began when Fr Liam O'Connell, a returned missionary from India, set up a meeting in a private house in Clonmel.[1] While conducting visitation on a parish mission in the town, a house named *The Aubeg* caught his eye. The Aubeg River ran close to Liam's home in North Cork and seeing the name on the house aroused his curiosity. The family were happy to meet him and in the course of an interesting conversation he suggested that they might continue it that night in the company of whatever neighbours they might chose to assemble for the occasion. That was the beginning of what we came to call *House Meetings*, the most effective instrument of our mission work in the past number of decades.

Later, Liam was on a mission in Dungarvan,[2] where he went a step further. During visitation he attended a meeting of the Town C ouncil, read a passage from the scriptures and reflected on its implications for both the council and for the mission. Thus began another dimension of the New Mission that ultimately embraced almost every group in the parish with the possible exception of the Bridge Club. We met the Junior Chamber of Commerce, Rotary Club, GAA, ICA, Muintir na Tíre, Macra na Feirme, Macra na Tuaithe, Civil Defence, Credit Unions, Teachers, Nuns, Brothers, Vincent de Paul, Legion of Mary – and that's not an exhaustive inventory.

Consolidation

Three highly significant missions that I was privileged to lead were in Cobh,[3] Clonakilty,[4] and Skibbereen.[5] Of all the missions I have been on, the Cobh mission was the most formative in the evolution of the New Mission. For a variety of reasons we were

1. St Mary's, Clonmel, 3-24 May 1970. Missioners: Frs Stan Mellett, Michael Clancy, Liam O'Connell.
2. Dungarvan, Co Waterford, 4 Oct – 1 Nov 1970. Missioners: Fr Stan Mellett, Michael Clancy, Liam O'Connell.
3. Cobh Cathedral, 18 April – 16 May 1971. Missioners: John J. Ó Ríordáin, Liam Hanley, Liam O'Connell, Richard Tobin, Peter Flannery.
4. Clonakilty, 26 Sept – 24 Oct 1971. Missioners: John J. Ó Ríordáin, Liam Hanley, Richard Tobin, William McGettrick.
5. Skibbereen 'Cathedral', 30 April – 28 May 1972. Missioners: John J. Ó Ríordáin, Richard Tobin, Peter Flannery.

under a lot of pressure and that pressure forced us to clarify our ideas and carefully plan every stage of the work. It was under that pressure too that I first experienced Religious Life, not as a juridical institution but as *a community of persons.* The support of the brethren in time of need breathed new life into me.

It was in Cobh that we perceived the four-week structure to be an integral feature of the new mission. It was also in Cobh that specific prayers and scripture readings were chosen to harmonise with the Morning Instruction themes. During the Cobh, Clonakilty and Skibbereen missions there was a consolidation of the creative ideas born in Clonmel and Dungarvan, together with the use of prayer formulae and hymns elaborated in Carrick-on-Suir/Carrickbeg.[6] By the time that these six missions had ended, the New Mission had taken on a definitive shape. Furthermore, since the six venues were not very different in population, we had a template for similar sized town missions throughout the country.

Visitation and House-Meetings
For generations past, blanket visitation of houses in urban areas was routine. In the early stages of the New Mission we visited six days a week. It soon became evident that Saturdays were unsuited to the task. Therefore the 'visiting week' ran from Monday to Friday. Each missioner was assigned approximately forty houses per day for visitation. Within that allotment he was expected to find two families who were willing to host housemeetings. After supper, he went in turn to the designated houses to chair and conduct the meetings. They began with a spontaneous prayer and a scripture reading and thereafter the agenda was open, although we did try to keep a certain focus around the question of what it meant to be church in that particular parish.

The whole experience was novel for the participants. It was probably their first experience of an open forum where a church-person was present as 'active listener' rather than 'defender of the faith.' Before getting down to anything constructive, people let off steam about church, priests, religious, com-

6. 7 Mar-4 Apr 1971. Missioners: Jim McGrath, Michael Clancy, Liam G. O'Carroll, Richard Tobin, Clement Mac Mánuis.

munity, family, youth, schools, politics, social services and just about everything else, including past missions and missioners. The numbers present at house meetings averaged about twenty. The lowest number in my experience was in a Dublin city centre parish where there was nobody but the couple who had kindly given me the use of their home. I later discovered that the neighbours had boycotted the meeting because the host and hostess had been streaking around the locality the previous week.

In the early 1970s the concept of house-meetings was a daring one. Priests were exposed to the possibility of criticism and that put a strain on the self-image. The vast majority of them were able to put the criticism in context; aware that it was not necessarily about them personally but about how people had experienced church over the years. Some priests, not many as far as I know, regretted having said 'yes' to the meetings, and indeed, looking back on it all now, I have a few regrets myself, but not too many, T. G. We were young and brash, on fire with a good idea and, speaking for myself, not always gifted with the degree of diplomacy and sensitivity that situations might have required at the time.

When I think of the New Mission and of house-meetings in particular I think of Cobh. The people there were wonderfully responsive. There was energy in the air. They had seen generations of strangers come and go at this port-town. The arrival of a few missioners wasn't going to frighten them. They engaged us in conversation on the streets, flocked to house meetings and community groups, openly propounding their views on church, state and planet. They enjoyed having an altogether new forum for expressing themselves, and more importantly, they felt they were being heard.

Four Categories

The first week in Cobh, described above, also included the children's mission. Some simple 'rounds' that had already been introduced by Fr Clement Mac Mánuis on previous missions were used to good effect and rang through the school playgrounds and town streets. Next followed a wonderful week with the young people. Fears were expressed initially to the effect that the young people wouldn't turn out. A debate on the matter ensued between bishop John Ahern and myself:

Bishop: 'Try them at a later hour in the morning.'

Ó Ríordáin: 'No! We'll have Mass for them at 7.00 o'clock.

Bishop: 'They won't come.'

Ó Ríordáin: 'Yes they will.'

There was an uncomfortable silence among the clergy gathered about the large dining room table. We had been advised before the meal never to contradict the bishop. Therefore here was a public challenge. The lines were drawn. Time would tell. It was tense. We waited.

At about 6.30 on the Monday morning of the teenagers' week, townspeople were awakened to the patter and tramp of many feet on the sidewalks. Crowds of young people were on their way to the seven o'clock Mass in the cathedral. Four hundred we counted and more, some of them not normally going to church or chapel. The adult population took note. The young had thrown down the challenge. The adults in their turn took it up and packed into the mission sessions: first the women, then the men. The pace was hectic but we were young, most of us anyhow. Towards the end of four gruelling weeks, when we were absolutely exhausted, a man walked up to me in 'the holy ground' and asked if I had enjoyed *my little holiday* in Cobh. I bit my lip.

Planning a New Mission

When requested to conduct a mission in olden times planning was minimal: just set the dates and find the personnel. Getting a priest to accept the New Mission was not that simple. Most priests were willing to give it a try and not many were as cynical as the parish priest in Cork city who told me he'd gladly accept the new because it couldn't be any worse than the old.

Planning a New Mission was more complex than simply having a word with the parish priest. The curates needed to be committed to it. The goodwill of the Religious Orders would need to be canvassed. With the passage of time more and more lay people were to get directly involved. Among the first lay recruits were the 'guardian angels' or guides who did magnificent work. During the visitation week they guided each of us to the area to be visited, directed us to the first house and then went along to house number two and three to alert the residents to our imminent visit. The presence of the 'guardian angel', usually in female form, set up a whole new social dynamic in terms of chatting to the neighbours, announcing the venue for the local house-meeting and in general raising the interest level within the community.

A generation later new teams of 'guardian angels' conducted the first phase of the mission by going two by two to every house in the parish distributing a specially prepared brochure with dates, times and other data relating to the mission. They were briefed and commissioned for this task one week before the arrival of the mission preachers. In the briefing they were recommended to play 'active listener' in the event of meeting irate parishioners and to make themselves scarce in the presence of irate dogs. This full visitation by parishioners themselves created a wonderful sense of involvement by the people in their own mission. A further development in lay involvement was the recruiting of local group leaders and notaries to run the house-meetings and report to a general assembly of priests and people at the weekend.

Preachers of the Word

A seminar held in Esker in 1972 produced an entirely new set of sermons that effectively replaced the old 1941 *Blue Book*. Mission booklets containing suitable prayers and hymns soon followed. With the advent of Evening Masses we came under a lot of pressure to incorporate Mass into the evening mission service. This we successfully resisted, maintaining that the primary purpose of the mission was to preach the Word of God in the context of popular prayer, hymn singing and Benediction. The Eucharist has always enjoyed its honoured place in our morning services, but in the popular mind, the 'missioner' essentially meant the 'preacher of the Word of God'.

Now that Counter Reformation spirituality is in a twilight zone, the centrality of the Word of God is once again dawning on the Catholic community. Of this centrality we have been forcefully reminded by the noted Dominican theologian, Yves Congar:

'I could quote a whole series of ancient texts,' he says, 'and saying more or less that if in one country Mass was celebrated for thirty years without preaching and in another there was preaching for thirty years without Mass, people would be more Christian in the country where there was preaching.'[7]

The Good News

With a view to encouraging the reading of the scriptures the New Mission personnel undertook to promote a popular readable text of the New Testament entitled *Good News for Modern Man*. The print was good and the illustrations bore a powerful message. We promoted it in every parish and bought copies in such quantity that the publishers, Collins of Edinburgh, told us that the Irish Redemptorists were their biggest customer worldwide.

The Mission Car

Coinciding with the introduction of the New Mission was the purchase of our first 'mission car' in Mt St Alphonsus. It took some of the hardship out of carrying personal belongings and large numbers of the *Good News*. It also created togetherness when setting out on a common task. Departure times were set but certain discrepancies surface in our response. Some were ready well ahead of time; others were trailing. More often than not I was among the stragglers:

> Wish I'd made that inventory.
> Am I forgetting anything?
> Sermons at the bottom,
> Ring binder with anecdotes,
> Bible and dictionary,
> Underwear round the radio.
> Yes, and the flex.
>
> Wonder what the digs are like:
> Short bed? Too soft? Dogs?

---

7. See: Congar, Yves, 'Sacramental Worship and Preaching' in *The Renewal of Preaching: Theory and Practice*, (*Concilium* 33) NY: Paulist 1968 pp 51-63, at p 62.

Oh, yes, the Crucifix!
I'll forget my head next.
Alarm clock in the shoe;
So far, so good. Notepaper;
A shower now and I'm right.

Blast it lads, give me a chance!
I am ready. Hell I'm stinking.
Yes I know it pulls across.
Hail Mary full of Grace ...
Mother of Perpetual Help, pray for us.
'This is Larry Gogan on Radio Two'
Ah *Jay* lads, give us a break![8]

Accommodation
Our first preference for accommodation during a parish mission
was the local presbytery and the last was a hotel. The former
afforded opportunity for better contact and pleasant converse
with brother-priests; the latter was counter productive by
putting the missioner outside the normal sphere of life of the
average parishioner. For myself, accommodation posed some
specific problems. They stem from being two metres in height,
having a weak back and being one of three Redemptorists
named O'Riordan all with the same Christian name and frequently at the same address.

The first thing on arrival therefore was to check the bed. If it
was too soft I slept on the floor; if too short, I pulled down the
mattress and stuffed some pillows in at the top. An end board
also sent me to the floor unless it was a double bed, in which
case I angled myself corner to corner. Then I had to explain that I
wasn't either of the other O'Riordans, just myself. One of the
three, Fr Seán, (*the* Fr O'Riordan) has now gone to his reward,
thus leaving two of us in Mt St Alphonsus to confuse the public:

You're welcome to the parish, Father!
Ah, Ó Ríordáin – a famous name:
You're nothing to, eh ...?
Three of you, is it? Well, well!

8. John J. Ó Ríordáin

Sure I know Kilbrin; very confusing at Christmas.
Kiskeam? That's in Boherbue parish isn't it?
Very good, *John J.* it shall be, then.
Anything you'd like by way of food?
What? A big man like you!
No wonder you're like a fishing rod.
And, by the way, the cabinet key is under the Bible.
Ah, on the floor, well 'pon your word!
A comfortable sleep they say.
The curate will take you to Pollnagaorach at nine.
You don't mind a bit of noise I suppose
It can be a bit rowdy after closing time.
We'll see you in the morning, then.
Good night and God Bless, eh, John J.[9]

A Memorable Occasion
A Mission in Killorglin, Co Kerry, stands out in my memory as a
wonderful occasion, a truly memorable and moving experience.
There was no meal when we arrived on the Saturday evening for
the simple reason that I had forgotten to mention it at the planning stage. Later that night I was ravenous and without changing out of my Redemptorist habit, ventured forth seeking something to devour. Some two or three hundred metres up the steep
street I spotted a chip shop. It wasn't far from the site of the platform where, in my teenage years, I had observed a puck goat
being not so solemnly crowned king on 10 August, the opening
day of the renowned Puck Fair.

It was now 16 March, the vigil of St Patrick's Day, and it was
also that hour of night when the disgorged pub clientele went in
search of savouries. The chip shop was crammed. At my entrance,
an uneasy silence descended on the establishment. I ordered fish
and chips and started to chat with one or two bystanders. Yes, I
was the missioner; a native of Kiskeam, just over the county
bounds. I'd be in Killorglin for a couple of weeks conducting the
parish mission. Gradually that silence gave way to a buzz of animated conversation, to handshakes all round, to sheer delight at
the presence of the missioner there among them in the chip
shop, and finally, to open competition for the privilege of pay-

9. Ó Ríordáin, John J.

ing for my simple purchase. I was overwhelmed by it all and having enjoyed the company and the food, returned to my room in the presbytery. It was then that *In the Chipper* flowed from an emotion-filled heart:

Hunger drove him to the street
As aged day dispensed its final hour
In the little hill-clung town
Unsung, safe for a he-goat
Annually crowned in orgy
And pedestalled aloft
His wayward kingdom to survey.

Yet, in a crowded chipper
The preacher heard a Gospel-word
Proclaimed, not in studied rhetoric
Nor from artistic podium
But in the eyes and from the hearts
Of young men and their fathers -
Keepers of an ancient faith.

He ate and supped for body's sake
While bread aplenty not of earthly fashion
They more broke, for joy that one
Should share their simple way.
And well the stranger knew
That one of Galilean's Twelve
Could not more welcome be that day.[10]

The sheer intensity of the New Mission, among other factors, led in time, to a certain retrenchment. The daring attempts at directly evangelising political, commercial, social and cultural groups was abandoned. Fear of house-meetings in some quarters led to the choice of more neutral venues such as community halls or clubrooms. The meetings too, changed in character. The open agenda of the house-meetings gave way to a more structured approach: certain questions to be addressed and explored; set 'cases' to be read out and debated. The inevitable human process of institutionalisation was overtaking the freedom and spontaneity of earlier times.

---

10. John J. Ó Ríordáin

The Solemn Novena

Almost immediately following on the emergence of the New Mission came another and more widely acclaimed initiative, that of The Solemn Novena. In 1943 Fr Matthew Meighan, an American Redemptorist chaplain to the US forces stationed in Northern Ireland during the Second World War, introduced the perpetual novena in honour of the Mother of Perpetual Help into Clonard Monastery, Belfast. Not long afterwards it was launched in Mt St Alphonsus, Limerick. As I remember it in the 1960s it was directed in turn by Fathers Anthony Mulvey and Pat McGowan, both then teaching in St Clement's College. Fr Vincent Kavanagh became Novena Director in 1971 and over the next several years under his dynamic leadership and meticulous planning the numbers making the novena leading up to the feast of the Mother of Perpetual Help on 27 June rose from an estimated two thousand to over 50,000. The June event became known widely as *The Solemn Novena* or *Festival of Faith*.

The Solemn Novena was not structured on the basis of a two-part daily attendance at morning Mass and Evening Devotions. Instead, the faithful were invited to come daily to a single session involving an amalgam of popular devotion, reconciliation, Mass, preaching and Holy Communion. Word of the Limerick phenomenon spread. Other Redemptorist churches in Ireland eagerly adopted the Solemn Novena and Fr Kavanagh was inundated with requests from Dublin, Carlow, Tuam, Holy Cross, the USA and elsewhere. All during this devotional extravaganza, Vincent Kavanagh never lost sight of the outreach to 'the widow and the orphan' by which term the Bible designates God's poor. From contributions of the faithful he organised an all-year-round distribution of food to people in need within the city and beyond. Though Fr Kavanagh is now in retirement, the Redemptorist Poor Campaign goes on and the latest figure from its centre of distribution at Mt St Alphonsus (2008) is that as many as 8,000 food hampers are delivered at Christmas and a further 250 per week throughout the year.

A Critical Reflection

As the Solemn Novena went from success to success a debate developed among ourselves concerning the respective merits of

Novena and Parish Mission in terms of pastoral strategy. We recognised both as expressions of the broad concept of mission, the one regional, the other local or parish-based. A Solemn Novena is an experience for a whole region particularly when an atmosphere of festival and pilgrimage take hold. Attempts to replicate that experience in a small or average parish with limited resources and personnel can sometimes disappoint.

An inappropriate substitution of parish novenas for parish missions short-sells the people of God by depriving them of the substantial preaching that is central to every parish mission. Even in this age of technology there is rarely anything more stirring than a well prepared and well delivered speech or sermon. Statements to the effect that the public are unwilling or unable to listen beyond a few minutes must be challenged. A few minutes can be far too long or far too short depending on the message and the messenger.

Smiles, Tears and the Grace of God

Much, if not most, of a missioner's work on a one-to-one basis is guarded either by the seal of confessional secrecy or a high degree of confidentiality. Occasionally a person will say 'you can tell my story,' but even then it is not always advisable or appropriate to do so. Other matters may be in the public domain. The few incidents recorded here will give a slight flavour of aspects of a missioner's life as yet unmentioned. Among the mildly amusing notices that came my way were a death notice that read 'Please pray for the repose of the soul of John Murphy who died at both Masses on Sunday', a Novena thanksgiving 'for successful sale of pub to the Mother of Perpetual Succour', and a letter requesting a 'Mass for the cows and you can include my wife'. In fairness to the author, the wording made sense in the circumstances and wasn't disrespectful to the man's wife who shared his husband's concern for the cows.

On a tragic note, I was on a mission in the pro-cathedral parish in Dublin during the 1974 bombing. Of the thirty or so killed on that fateful day, seven were killed on the sidewalk outside the door of our digs, Neary's Hotel in Parnell St. I understand that the man in the shop beside us had his head blown off and it was next day before the discovery of another body that had been blasted on to a flat roof. May God have mercy on all who died in the Dublin and Monaghan bombings, and in his mercy grant a spirit of repentance to the perpetrators of the crimes.

Then there was the man who rushed into the church late one night as I was finishing confessions. It was my custom to sit in the box for a little while after the last confession had been heard, just in case somebody trying to muster up courage was still hesitant. The church door burst open, a man walked straight up to my confession-box and arrived in breathless. It took me a while to get the drift of his introduction. He spoke of 'that woman on the television'. I couldn't help him on that one as I had been in the box all night. He had been up in the pub enjoying a quiet Saturday night drink until 'that nun' came on the screen. And with the sight of her, he had no peace, not until he had abandoned his pint on the counter and his friends in the bar and come down to make his confession, something he hadn't done for many years. He couldn't remember who 'that woman' was but she was on the *Late Late Show*. As it transpired, 'that woman' was Mother Teresa of Calcutta. It was a beautiful ending to a long night in the *box*.

During the Tramore mission there was an unusually heavy fall of snow. I had occasion to celebrate the early Mass on Sunday morning. Clad in heavy overcoat and shod in wellingtons, I trudged along to church. On the far side of the street I observed a lone man coming in my direction. When he got within shouting distance he called across the deserted street, 'There's milk in O'Connors!' I suspect that the kindly young man thought me to be a father, but I was only a Holy Father and had no such concerns.

Among the housebound whom I visited on the outer fringes of the Sliabh Luachra highlands in south Munster was a pleasant elderly woman living on her own. We chatted for a while. I then gave her Holy Communion and we prayed a little more. As I was about to depart she put a five pound note into my hand, a goodly sum at the time, and said, 'Father will you say Mass for me?' 'I will,' said I. With some emphasis she continued, 'Say it for myself now Father, because I have no one belonging to me only nieces and nephews, and your *sowl* could be *lepping* below in hell and all they'd want to know was how much money you have left in the bank.' *O Sapientia!*

Pastoral Dynamite: (a) Contraception
By the time the New Mission and the house meetings emerged at the beginning of the 1970s the contraception debate was reaching fever pitch. It came up at house meetings, in the confessional, in conversation with clergy and laity, just about everywhere. If contraception was the great sin of the laity, being 'soft on contraception' was the unforgivable sin of the missioner.

The debate weighed heavily upon us. It was stressful, tense, and ugly at times, too, because it meant difficulties with fellow priests. Most of all, it was painful in the confessional. We could cope with being suspended from priestly ministry much as we might be annoyed by it. But what were we to say in the confessional to people who were obviously good, decent, prayerful Christian parents, earnestly trying to live their married and family life within the bounds of their Catholic tradition but who occasionally fell short of the stated ideal? We consulted theologians, studied the 'Washington Declaration' and statements on the issue by different hierarchies around the world. From such reading and study it was patently obvious that there were various and benign pastoral interpretations of *Humanae Vitae* and by the Grace of God many of us were not afraid to apply them.

Having a reliable pastoral theology, however, did not save us entirely. There always remains in confessional practice the issue of what the confessor *said*, and what he is *reported to have said*. Because of the seal of confession we had no redress against the accusation of being 'soft on contraception' and we remained in a vulnerable position, particularly in terms of being engaged for further work in the parish or diocese. The debate eventually subsided as people either ignored the issue or under the guidance of the Holy Spirit found a satisfactory *modus vivendi*.

It was during that time that one of our Dutch confrères got an eye-opener from a lovely young married couple. They tried and failed to live by the strict letter of the law that the missioner had laid down for them. They then returned to the missioner with an interesting proposition. 'Father,' said the young man, 'my wife and I have tried to live by your guidance but we find that we cannot. However, having discussed the matter among ourselves we have decided that you can take my wife for one week and see if you are capable of living by the standards you are setting for us.'

Even in the streets or on public transport we weren't free from the contraception debate. At a bus stop between Limerick and Ennis a man boarded, looked around, spotted me in full clerical garb complete with Roman collar, and planked himself down beside me. He wasn't drunk, but he was in good talking form and proceeded to give me the benefit of his views on contraception and the priesthood in a voice that everybody could plainly hear. 'I had seven sons,' said he, 'and I didn't contracept any one of them. And not one of them became a priest. And,' said he with emphasis, 'that's where the money is!' Since that afternoon, I ceased using clericals when travelling.

Aware of the tortuous debate, Donal Foley resorted to 'the safety valve of the nation' to bring a little light relief. In his column 'Man bites Dog' in *The Irish Times*, he wrote:

In a Pastoral Letter read at all the Masses in the city on Sunday, Bishop Lucey [of Cork] condemned the disk-parking system as 'contrary to Catholic teaching.' The new scheme, the bishop said, was in direct opposition to the teaching of the encyclical *Automobilis Progressio*. It could lead to the city being overrun by disk jockeys.

Particularly in this season of Lent, Dr Lucey went on, it was desirable that Cork motorists should practice abstinence from driving, and leave their cars at home. 'The primary function of motoring,' he said, 'is the transportation of children, and only secondary for personal pleasure.'

The bishop pointed out that, for those Catholics who were forced to use their cars, the local diocese provided special car parks, mainly attached to Catholic churches, which had been approved and blessed by the hierarchy.[11]

---

11. *The Irish Times*, 18 March 1975

Pastoral Dynamite: (b) The Troubles

The conflict in the North overshadowed almost all of my working mission life. Missioners, and I include myself among them,
frequently addressed the topic. We didn't always find the most
appropriate words in an attempt to apply the gospel to the situation in hand. I'll long remember the night that I addressed the
state of affairs in Ireland as I saw them. A well-dressed gentleman, infuriated by my utterances, pursued me into the sacristy
where we verbally battled it out for a considerable time. Because
of the inaccurate manner in which the gentleman was attempting to quote me, I threatened him with libel. On returning to the
presbytery that night I described my assailant to the parish
priest. He took a delightful fit of laughing and informed me that
the person whom I had threatened with libel was the local judge.
We drank to that!

CHAPTER EIGHT

From Cork to Alaska (1974)
'All de way by bus'

Luxembourg

It was in 1973 that Ireland acquired membership of the European Economic Community, now the European Union. To meet the needs of this new situation the Bishop of Luxembourg requested the Irish Redemptorists to accept a chaplaincy to the Irish and English speaking civil servants in the new European Parish that he had established. Jim McGrath, our provincial superior, sent me to assess the situation and I spent two interesting weeks with the parishioners who were mostly new arrivals from Ireland. On my return home I presented a positive report and Fr Anthony Mulvey was appointed to the post. It was a good choice. Anthony was not only fluent in several languages but was a fine preacher, an efficient administrator and a renowned raconteur.

The most significant memory from my own visit to Luxembourg is that of coming to terms with the idea of a married clergy. At the time there was an Irishman who had resigned from the priestly ministry and taken to himself a wife. Both were working in the ranks of the EEC civil service. It was plain that this former Maynooth professor was the acknowledged, if unofficial, leader of the Irish community in the city. Furthermore, being the perfect gentleman that he was, it seemed appropriate that he rather than a stranger like myself should preside at the Sunday Eucharist.

An Unrealised Ambition

Whether it was my success in Luxembourg or not, my yen for travel was to get another surprise outing before very long. Such opportunities were welcome because I always had an interest in travel, in exploring the big wide world. As a child I used to look out the front door of our house and wonder at that world. My mother had told me that there were five oceans and seven seas but I found it difficult to fit them all in between our front door and the horizon at the top of Dromscarra, a distance of less than three kilometres as the crow flies.

I had an aunt, Mary Murphy, from the Shamrock House who taught school in England. From time to time she would bring home old class texts that were a Godsend in the early 1940s. My mother loved them and used to read them to me: stories of Greece and Rome, of Egypt and Mesopotamia, and of the Seven Wonders of the World, which included 'the temple, gates, and hanging gardens of Babylon.' The Babylonian wonders fascinated me, perhaps because in some curious way that ancient city and empire wasn't far removed from the home of my childhood. You see, John Murphy from Kiskeam Upper, had served in the British army and one of his proudest boasts concerned a stint in Mesopotamia: 'I slept in the Garden of Eden, I did.'

Nor was John Murphy the only Kiskeam man to travel far. A namesake of his, Jack the Soldier, had been in India. The Hickey boys from The Lane were on a whaling expedition to the Antarctic, Dan-Pad-Óg Lane was a member of the 1909 Bernier expedition to the High Arctic, and my granduncle Patrick Murphy who went to Australia towards the end of the 19th century was elected first Mayor of Cooma, now the main town in the Snowy Mountain region of New South Wales. Several others made their fortunes as cowboys and shepherds in the wilds of Oregon, but nobody can remember if a fortune was made by the man who went picking bananas in Mexico.

The likelihood of making an impact on the travel exploits of Kiskeamers was slim enough when I was not assigned to the foreign missions in 1964. My appointment to teach religion and sociology in the Limerick VEC in 1968 opened a chink, through which I saw a remote possibility of crossing the Atlantic. The staff and students of the Marine Radio School had knowledge of the seafaring world and I began to explore the possibility of getting a summer job as a deck hand on a grain ship plying between Limerick and the Great Lakes.

My exploratory negotiations for a temporary career in the country's mercantile navy were shelved in the autumn of 1969 when our successful palace revolution overthrew the ancient regime and set the Irish province of the Redemptorists full steam ahead in implementing the tenets of the Second Vatican Council. There was a new freedom in the air and since my VEC chaplaincy qualified me for associate membership of the Irish Students Union, I was able to get a cheap ticket and in June 1970 flew to New York, my first time in an aeroplane. There I got a two-month Greyhound bus ticket for $132 and travelled over 10,000 miles in the US, Canada and Mexico. During that outing I did a few days work here and there, frequently slept on the bus, slept rough at the Greyhound depot in New Orleans, and re-turned safely to Ireland. That was my Grand Tour. I had no fur-ther plans or even ambitions to visit the New World.

A Research Assignment

Towards the end of 1973 a novel assignment landed on my desk. One morning in December, Jim McGrath came almost casually to my room in Esker and said, 'J. J. would you ever hop across the Atlantic, take a look at the course offerings in the various universities, find out where the really good ones are and report back.' I agreed and Jim was gone as swiftly as he had entered. I parted with my 84-year-old father in Kiskeam in the small hours of 16 January 1974 and had dinner in Boston that evening with Murt Culloty, his cousin and life-long friend.

In Boston I thought out a work strategy. At each place visited I'd inquire about course offerings in local colleges and universi-ties. Then, almost by way of an afterthought, I'd ask if there were any courses across the North American continent that might be worth looking at. In time this second question would be the makings of the research. For transport I chose the Greyhound bus and bought an unlimited travel ticket. Three months and 15,000 miles later, I stepped off the bus in New York City at 11.45 pm. My ticket expired at midnight. It was good value for $165. Later, back in Ireland, I submitted my report on the educational opportunities on offer in North America and happily, several confrères made use of it in planning sabbaticals.

Naturally, I took a look at what was available in the Boston area, then on to New York, Phidalphia, Washington DC and Pittsburg. By that time I had learned that the East Coast was con-servative, the West Coast liberal, and that Toronto was leading all North America as a centre of theological study. On 27

January therefore, I set my face towards that great city travelling along the shores of Lake Erie to the cities of Erie, Buffalo and Niagara Falls in NY State and St Catharine's on the Canadian side of the frontier. Here an Algonquin fur-trapper boarded the bus and sat beside me. He was recovering from a broken leg and not yet free of the crutches. The fact that he was illiterate made him feel uncomfortable in an urban setting and was glad to be heading back to his wigwam on a frozen lake. His geography left something to be desired also because at the mention of Ireland he said, 'Ah, far off. You come all *de* way by bus?' As an alternative to a lecture on the Atlantic Ocean I switched to the weather. It had begun to snow at Niagara Falls and by now everything was white in St Catharine's. It would be six weeks and several thousand miles later before setting foot on the bare ground.

Toronto, Ottawa, Detroit, Chicago, Notre Dame

Mild winters are not welcome in Canada, especially in Ottawa where the canal is said to be the longest skating rink in the world and much used by the citizens on their way to and from work. My confrère, Robert McGoran, then studying in the Canadian capital, said that he had not yet taken to skating his way to college. In Toronto I stayed with the Redemptorists. The community reflected the city's cosmopolitan nature. The Toronto School of Theology (TST) deserved its reputation, being as it was the stamping ground of Gregory Baum, Bernard Lonergan, Leslie Dewart and a plethora of world famous scholars.

In Chicago I was met at the Greyhound depot by Joe Corbett and later joined by Liam O'Connell. Both confrères were studying in the city and supplied me with relevant information on Loyola University and other centres of interest. I stayed in our monastery of St Michael's in the Old Town Triangle where Joe was based. At that time the vicinity was positively dangerous but since then it has undergone urban renewal. At South Bend, Indiana, Desmond Hopkins from Tuam was waiting for me and from there we drove straight to Notre Dame university. The journey through the flat snowcovered terrain gave me a taste of what it might be like to get lost in a blizzard. Even under a blanket of snow the university buildings had an air of opulence, set as they are on a twelve-hundred acre campus. On entering the university I felt a bit lost but it wasn't long before professor Bob Gorman came on the scene and told me that his grandfather was one of the Gormans of Meal, a wellknown family in my native parish of Boherbue, Co Cork.

Indianapolis, Davenport, Des Moines, Omaha

Indiana Trailways did not honour Greyhound tickets. I therefore paid $16 for the next leg of my journey from Indianapolis to Davenport where the expansive Mississippi river separates Illinois from Iowa. A warm welcome from Ed Morgan, the Redemptorist superior, kept my spirits afloat until reaching Omaha, Nebraska on Sunday 10 February where our confrère Fr Delort made me equally welcome. At that time, Delort was reading for a master's degree in Pastoral Ministry at Creighton Jesuit University. Since our new Pastoral Centre in Marianella, Dublin offered a somewhat similar programme to that at Creighton, I arranged for a meeting with the chancellor to discuss the possibility of an affiliation for Marianella. It was my hope that such an arrangement might open the way for the mutual recognition of credits towards a degree. My proposal met with a favourable response from the chancellor but John O'Donnell, the Director of the Marianella Pastoral Centre, being more of an administrator than an innovator, did not pursue it.

Mid-West Farming

In terms of geography I was now in the heart of mid-west farmland were 'the corn is as high as an elephant's eye' and frequently growing on fourteen feet of topsoil. Cattle herds numbering tens of thousands were fed on grass and finished on unthreshed maize (corn on the cob). Omaha, Nebraska and Sioux City, Iowa, among others owe their very existence to the trade. Their stock yards (marts) are probably the largest in North America and handle millions of cattle each year. For the convenience and safety of the dealers, the yards are equipped with an elaborate overhead array of metal foot walks and ramps .

It was close to the Sioux City stock yards that a couple in late middle age boarded the bus. They had just retired from farming and were taking a short holiday before getting down to building a retirement home. The husband who was the chief spokesperson had views not only on farming but on many other matters as well. For example, he did not take kindly to the idea of couples focusing on the appearance of the house rather than on the quality of living, and the placing of undue restrictions on children lest they damage the rug (carpet) or the furniture. This gentleman and his wife had other values. As he put it, 'When I build *ma* house, I'm *gonna* let the kids come in. And when one rug is *wore* out we *git anither.*'

Having parted with the farming couple I got into conversation with a Lutheran woman. I'm afraid we both ganged up on a very vocal fundamentalist lady and allowed ourselves to indulge in a bit of leg-pulling. The hastily cobbled alliance between Martin Luther's disciple and myself more or less fell asunder when she asked me to compare Ireland and the USA. I suggested that the food in Ireland was superior to the general run of what was available in her country. She was flabbergasted and on recovering her speech suggested that I mustn't have been going to the right places – you bet I wasn't! She then and there extended a *Ceád míle fáilte* to her farmhouse where I was promised full and plenty of the best.

Minneapolis-St Paul and Harry Walsh

At the bus depot in Minneapolis there were two Redemptorists to greet me: Harry Walsh, whom I had known since Juvenate days in Limerick, and Ernest (Ernie) Larsen who was known to me from his writings, notably the catchy titles, *Good Old Plastic Jesus* and *You Try Love and Ill' try Ajax*. Ernie is also the author of *And Tomorrow We ...*, a book on the squalor of the Vietnam War which was then raging. That book drew down on him the wrath of people in high places.

Harry worked in one of the poorest parishes in the city where he was well loved by the people. An early manifestation of the new spirit of freedom in the post Vatican II church was the resignation of many priest and Religious from the ministry. Harry's parish was now understaffed due to the recent departure of two priests. This annoyed the parish clerk whose priority was efficiency rather than any moral niceties, 'I don't mind if they go down to Chicago for a dirty weekend, but to be back on the job.'

At thirty minutes past midnight I bid farewell to Harry and boarded a bus bound for Winnipeg in 'sunny Manitoba of the hundred thousand lakes.' We travelled north west through Fargo and Grand Forks, crossed the Canadian frontier and sped swiftly towards our destination. The sight of so many feed-lots and grain silos and little else indicated that beneath the snowcap lay one vast prairie cornfield. On 12 February I had purchased a pair of polarised glasses in Sioux City. The time had come to use them.

The Filioque Controversy by Taxi

It was about one o'clock in the afternoon of Sunday 17 February, when we reached Winnipeg. The city was enwrapped in a clean blanket of fresh snow. I hailed a taxi, a rare gesture on my part, as I usually find a suitable bus or check the map to see if my destination is within walking distance. On discovering that I was a priest of the Roman church, the taxi-man, a Greek-Orthodox Christian, opened up an age old controversy between the Greek and Latin churches.

The theological dispute centred on the Holy Trinity and the inclusion by the Western or Latin church of the word *Filioque* ('and the Son') which had not been part of the Creed as promulgated at Council of Nicene in 325AD. The dispute is concretised in Michael Cerularius, Patriarch of Constantinople, storming out of a meeting with the Roman delegations in Sancta Sophia on that fateful day in July 1054. The emotion surrounding that ancient controversy was still bubbling in Winnipeg and I only wished that in our Western church we took as keen an interest in knowing our faith. From the dizzy and emotionally draining heights of Trinitarian theology we moved on to safer ground. The taxi-man told me that he kept huskies and with that there was a tacit agreement to put the *Filioque* on the back burner.

To get to the front door of our monastery I trudged through a depth of snow. Once inside, however, the welcome was warm; homely too, as it was a Fr O'Connor who admitted me and he in turn introduced me to the rector, Fr Murphy.

Western Canada

Geologists are aware that the Pacific Ocean visited Saskatchewan and Manitoba on three separate occasions over the millennia, the first leaving salt deposits and the second oil fields. About a hundred million years ago the west erupted, threw up the Rockie Mountains and put manners on the Pacific. Finally, about 10,000 years ago, at the height of the ice age, humans crossed the ice-bridge over the Bering Straits to become the first Canadians.

The casting up of the Rockies has tamed the Pacific to some extent but there is as yet an untamed streak in the Canadian temperament that is positively refreshing. The country is divided from its neighbour by a line on the map but the difference is as clear as Irish and English. At the time of my visit to Edmonton, Alberta, the Redemptorists of that area were led by the highly popular Fr Grattan Feehan whose ancestors came from Tipperary. Grattan told me that he and Jim McGrath once compared notes on distances within their respective territories. While Jim McGrath could visit all his Irish monasteries on a round trip of less than five hundred miles, Grattan Feehan travelled up to eight thousand miles on a similar venture in Western Canada. And that was only the territory of the provincial of the Edmonton Province; there were also provincials in Toronto and Quebec plus a Ukranian Rite provincial.

Mrs Gallagher the Eskimo

Another member of the community, Fr Edward (Ed) Kennedy, was heavily involved in the political life of Edmonton. He stood for the local elections, won a seat and was making his presence felt in the city. Ed was also active in many areas of church life: Director of the Catholic Information Centre for the archdiocese, chairman of the Association of Western Priests, and a strong advocate of married clergy and the ordination of women. Fr Neil Corbett, then on our parish mission team, told me that when he was on mission in the wild North Western Territory the weather was so bad that on a particular morning only one woman and her children turned up at church. She was an Eskimo. The priest introduced himself and the dark lady in turn introduced herself as 'Mrs Gallagher!' She and her Irish husband had settled in the area where they were happily rearing their seven children.

Oh dear!

My short stay in Edmonton provided one of the most embarrassing moments in my life. Most of the confrères were gathered in the community room watching the news or some such programme. A curious little object on a table caught my eye. I picked it up and wondered what it might be. Rather frequently, in an absentminded sort of way, I would press the colourful array of little buttons. Nobody said anything. One by one the confrères quietly departed from the room until eventually there was only one confrère left with me. After a while he asked if I was interested in the particular programme on the screen. 'Not at all!' I replied. He then politely asked me to pass him the remote control. 'Where is it?' said I. 'In your hand!' said he. Although I am six-foot-seven inches tall and fourteen stone weight, I could have disappeared through a keyhole!

The Lure of the North Country

It was now Friday 22 February and I had been travelling for five weeks. My Boston strategy, if we may so call it, was proving satisfactory as a research method and I had already accumulated a considerable amount of useful information. The snowy conditions gave the impression that I was further north than I actually was. A glance at the map indicated that Edmonton, Galway and Dublin were on the same latitude. I was frozen, yes, but not in the Arctic, not yet anyway. It was clear to me, though, that if a long-cherished dream of getting there was ever to be realised, this was the opportune moment. I rang the bus depot in Edmonton and inquired if there was a service going north at that time of year. The receptionist said that there was a bus leaving at midnight on the two thousand-mile journey to Fairbanks, Alaska, and that it would get there in a few days. I was on it.

The driver announced the main centres along the route: Grand Prairie, Dawson Creek, Fort Nelson, Fort St John, Watson Lake, Whitehorse, Haines Junction, Beaver Creek, Tok Junction, Fairbanks. It was not that we had the same driver for the entire journey. That would have been beyond the bounds of human endurance. Ah, but what a journey! Exotic names, exotic places spread over Alberta, British Colombia, the Yukon Territory and Alaska; two thousand miles of snow, ice, forest, tundra; two thousand miles of spectacular scenes of desolate wilderness and mountain ranges with peaks disappearing into the heavens and scarcely a soul to praise the designer.

For some peculiar reason I had always considered Dawson Creek to be *ultima thule*, the very end of the world. Yet, it was only the second break in the long journey north to Alaska. It may not have been the North Pole but it felt like it. During a two-hour break I made my way to a lovely new church and monastery built by the Redemptorist community but now transferred to the Oblates of Mary Immaculate, the apostles of the Northcountry. There I celebreated Mass, had breakfast and chatted with Terence Conway, William Devlin and Walter Doherty, the latter having grown up across the fields from the Four Elms, a landmark pub in Drumbanna, near Limerick city.

Alaska Highway
The road linking Dawson Creek in British Columbia with Fairbanks in Alaska is fifteen hundred miles long and known as The Alaska Highway. It was constructed in 1942 as a rough surfaced but functional military road that ran up hill and down dale through tundra, forest and mountain. After World War II, in 1946, it was opened to the public.

Between Dawson Creek and Fort St John we entered the valley of the Great Peace River. The bridge that spanned the ice-capped river was a massive and thoroughly scary-looking wooden structure made of tall pine trees criss-crossed and lashed together. A fervent prayer split the clouds as we approached this contraption, for although it was said that in general these bridges were reliable there was always the fear that bridge, bus and passengers would end up in the deep ravine at the bottom of which might be the peace of the grave. In fact it was not long after my journey that one such bridge over the Great Peace River did collapse.

Fellow travellers on the bus were mostly indigenous peoples going about their business and conversing in their native tongue or sometimes in heavily accented English. My experience of bus drivers in North America was, almost without exception, one of mature men with easy and pleasant personalities. In Western Canada and Alaska they excelled themselves. The Alaska

Highway offered one panoramic view after another. The sheer proportions, the continuity of great mountain ranges, the individual massive snow-white peaks, and the seemingly endless forests were enough to take my breath away. And then there was the silence.

> Were you ever out in the Great Alone,
> When the moon was awful clear,
> And the icy mountains hemmed you in
> with a silence you most could *hear*.[1]

In one day's travelling we covered a full three hundred miles, the length of Ireland, and nobody got on or off that bus. This was a desolate land. Trees and mountains, yes. People, no. Towns and villages were few and far between and passengers were more often than not numbered in single digits. I was told of an Irish girl who became a nun and worked among the scattered peoples of this land. When she lay dying somebody said to her, 'Are you worried?' 'No,' she replied calmly, 'No, I am at peace. I gave up Ireland and if God doesn't give me heaven for that, well ...' Even after a couple of days I could appreciate her sentiments.

The townships along the highway despite their evocative names were in reality little more than trading posts. One by one they came into view, each in its frozen isolation: Taylor, Fort St John, Wonowon, Trutch, Prophet River, Fort Nelson, Steamboat, Muncho Lake, Coal River, Lower Post, Watson Lake, Swift River, Teslin, Johnsons Crossing, Jakes Corner, Whitehorse, Champagne, Haines Junction, Kluane, Burwash Landing, Northway Junction, Tok, Tanacross, Delta Junction, Richardson, Fairbanks. Many of these villages are named after explorers, trappers, engineers, prospectors; and, have you guessed it, Wonowon is so named because it is mile 101 on the Alaska Highway.

Fort St John is the oldest settlement in mainland British Columbia. The North West Company established a fort there in the 1790s under the direction of the explorer Sir Alexander Mackenzie, the first white man to travel from the Great Lakes to

1. Service, R., 'The Shooting of Dan McGrew' in *Songs of the Sourdough*, p. 59.

the Pacific coast. It was the churning rapids of the Yukon River prompted the name Whitehorse for a settlement south of Lake Lebarge. The indigenous peoples, unacquainted with horses, called it *Klil-has*, meaning very bad. Kluane Lake is exactly what *klooahnee-munn* means, large fish lake.

The Yukon

As Sunday morning, 24 February, dawned we were passing close to the source of the Yukon River and thereafter we followed its valley where the men had 'moiled for gold'. The river's name, *yukonna* means great river in Athabaskan and it is certainly all that. There is still gold in the area but not in commercial quantities. We paused at Gold Horn Mine where tourists come to pan the icy waters in summertime. Although they are guaranteed to get some gold for their few dollars investment, making a fortune is not their goal. The same spirit that drew the men of '98 to the Yukon probably draws those modern panners as well:

> Yet it isn't the gold that I'm wanting
> So much as just finding the gold.
> It's the great, big, broad land 'way up yonder,
> It's the forests where silence has lease;
> It's the beauty that thrills me with wonder;
> It's the stillness that fills me with peace.[2]

At some unspecified stage on the arctic journey I made friends with a young man from Sonora, Mexico. There wasn't much of a choice for either of us, for even though it was the regular and only bus service to that part of the world, we were often the only passengers. Emilio Dabdoub was a thoughtful young man, one of a family of three boys and not yet married. He and a brother ran a small shop in Nogales on the Mexican-Arizona border. Emilio thought it best to do his travelling while single. Furthermore it gave him the opportunmity of meeting girls from other countries before making a final marriage choice because, once married, Emilio was determined to be a faithful husband. When I met him he had already done a lot of travelling in the

---

2. Service, R., 'The Spell of the Yukon,' in *Songs of the Sourdough*, p. 25.

USA and Canada. Now it would be Alaska and then Europe. It was, he said, probably the only major trip in his life.

The journey from Edmonton to Whitehorse had taken 34 hours and covered well over a thousand miles. Conditions were getting colder by the mile and I was continually like an icicle. Since I had no suitable clothing for temperatures of forty and fifty degrees below zero and worse, I tried to ward off some of the cold by putting on every stitch in my suitcase but it made little difference. Emilio and I walked the snowy streets of Whitehorse, sightseeing if you don't mind! Rarely did I feel so miserable or lonely or so far from home. I had come to the Yukon, then, to freeze. And yet, I knew deep down that I would be back in Ireland in a couple of months time telling people how much I enjoyed it all. We took photographs in front of the romantically named White Horse Inn. Our next point of interest was the old railway terminus. During the Gold Rush at the end of the 19th century, a railway ran from Skagway over the 2,900 foot summit of White Pass, along by Lake Bennett following the Klondike trail and so to Whitehorse.

> We landed in wind-swept Skagway.
> We joined the weltering mass;
> Clambouring over their outfits,
> Waiting to climb the Pass.[3]

In 1897, White Pass was named in honour of Sir Thomas White, the Canadian minister for the interior. It was at Bennett that the gold prospectors built boats to carry them down the Yukon River, and at Miles Canyon Jack London made his living piloting groups through its boiling flood.

The intrepid Emilio did not share any sense of my self pity in the cold. He had an agenda that involved every step of the way. This young farmer-cum-shopkeeper of 26 years of age did not fit into the stereotype image of the Mexican. He was well organised, kept a daily diary and each morning would note the external temperature to be 'telling my grandchildren'. Respect, good manners, generosity, natural grace, all seemed to be second nature to him. At the end of our walkabout Emilio went to his

---

3. Service, R., 'The Trail of Ninety-Eight' in *Collected Verse of Robert Service*, Vol 1, p. 179.

digs at the WWCA in 4th avenue; I to the Oblates in Steele St. We did not meet again until reboarding the bus.

It was good to step inside a warm Oblate house. So warm was it that I decided to check the internal temperature. To my amazement it was only 56 degrees Fahrenheit, but it seemed like a furnace by comparison with the cold outside. There was a great welcome from Fr Brian Kearns from Dublin and his Canadian confrère Br Guy Levaque. Guy was five-foot tall and slight in build. As we stood side by side somebody remarked to him, 'I don't know who the fellow with you is, but he looks like a body guard.'

Poustinia

The Oblates told me that there was an Irishman at Maryhouse, a residence occupied by four nuns and a lay man, Seán (Jack) O'Callaghan from Cork and a classmate of my revered friend, Fr James Good. The Russian foundress of the community, Countess Catherine de Huec (later Catherine Doherty), had done inspirational work in the slums of New York and became more widely known as the author of *Poustinia*, a fine book on her native Russian spirituality.

There was a sequel to my visit. In the early winter of 1974 I wrote a note of thanks to the community expressing my support for their apostolate. The letter eventually made its way to the foundress who wrote to me as follows on 1 February 1975 from her headquarters at Madonna House in Cumbermere, Ontario:

Dearly Beloved Father and Friend,

Thank you so very much for your lovely letter that you have written to the Yukon. I was sorry that you didn't pass by Madonna House, and we were all enthused about your being a kitchen porter; more power to you!

I hope that if you ever come back to Canada you will be coming to Madonna House where you will meet many of your countrymen. Then again it seems to me as if you have been here.

Anyhow, blessed and joyous New Year.

In unity of love and prayers,

Catherine

Catherine Doherty

The letter is treasurable in itself, not least because I believe that one day Catherine will be canonised.

The Sourdough Rendezvous

By good fortune my stay in Whitehorse coincided with the high-light of annual festivity, the *Yukon Sourdough Rendezvous*. The festival is rooted in the Gold Rush days. The name derives from the custom of prospectors and trappers carrying a 'starter' of sour dough, i.e. flour mixed with yeast and beer which fermented and lasted for days or weeks. It was baked in pancake form as need arose. In Whitehorse, during the Rendezvous, sourdough breakfasts were all the rage.

Looking at it from an Irish perspective, one might conceive of the whole event as an amalgam of the Rose of Tralee, Puck Fair and Listowel Races, with Fleadh Ceoil na hÉireann thrown in for good measure. The ladies dress in period costume. The men grow beards and the Junior Chamber acting as mock police are liable to arrest, fine or jail men found without beard or badge. Among the many activities are snowmobile and ski-doo races, dog sledge racing, an air display, ice-rink displays and packlifting competitions.

If the Babylonian Empire wasn't far from Kiskeam folklore in my young days, neither was the Yukon. A relative of mine, Dan Murphy from Ballydesmond, tried his luck in the High North before returning to Sliabh Luachra and opening a pub. The only name by which it was ever known is Klondikes. Another reason for familiarity with the Yukon is the popularity of Robert Service's chronicling of that era in poems and recitations. Literate or otherwise, most people were familiar with *The Cremation of Sam McGee, The Shooting of Dan McGrew*, and the behaviour of 'the lady that's known as Lou'.

A newcomer to the Yukon is called a *Cheechako*, a word derived from Chinook, the *lingua franca* of the Pacific Northwest for both traders and locals. It is a compound of *t'shi* meaning new and *Nootka chako* meaning to arrive. At Whitehorse, Cheechakos are swiftly introduced to Sam Magee's Cabin, which is about as authentic as a Killarney leprechaun. Sam is a literary construct embodying the distilled essence of many a prospector's experience of a Yukon winter:

Now there sat Sam, looking cool and calm,
in the heart of the furnace roar,
And he wore a smile you could see a mile,
and he said: 'Please close the door.
It's fine in here; but I greatly fear
you'll let in the cold and storm –
Since I left Plumtree, down in Tennessee,
it's the first time I've been warm'.[4]

Lake Lebarge, on the margin of which is set the scene of Sam Magee's cremation, is an expansive stretch of the Yukon river. I saw it for the first and only time at 10.30 am on Monday, 25 February courtesy of Brian Kearns. After a drive 'over the Dawson Trail' we had a brisk walk not just on 'the marge of Lake Lebarge' but right out over the lake itself, which was then frozen to a depth of approximately five feet. And just to make things more authentic, two beautiful dashing huskies came, as it were, out of nowhere and played and frolicked about us.

Huskies, Snow Birds and Ice Leprechauns
Huskies are part and parcel of the Northland. They are strong and serve many purposes. My Greek Orthodox taxi driver told me that his Siberian huskie weighed seven stone and when harnessed the children could hitch him to a toboggan and drive through the winter snows. Skidoos and snowmobiles have tended to replace the huskies but the huskies are more dependable in rough terrain, and there's plenty of that in the Yukon. It is true that the animals can be frisky and somewhat excitable so that failure on the part of a lead dog to take the proper signals can cause the pack to turn in on itself in futile savaging.

The dogs are integral to the sporting world too, and nowhere more so than at the Sourdough Rendezvous. 'Going to the races' at the Sourdough means above all, going to the dog-sledge races. The arena is the river. If Ottawa claims the longest skating rink in the world, Whitehorse can claim the longest racecourse. Like Lake Lebarge it is frozen deep and offers unlimited facilities for trucks, tractors, cars, tents and the assembled multitude.

4. Service, R., 'The Cremation of Sam McGee' in *Songs of the Sourdough*, p. 69.

At the Sourdough races I watched the teams take off smoothly as the mushers ran alongside or after the sledges and then jumped aboard. The sight was verging on the mystical. The vision soon faded from view because the fifteen-mile race took them more than seven miles down river to the turning point. Their reappearance on the homeward journey was a pathetic, even a tearful sight. The steeming animals strained on the last ounce of energy to drag the sledge while the musher, once again running alongside encouraged the exhausted dogs with sweet words and comforting sounds as they approached the finishing post.

When the *Snow Birds* flew in over Whitehorse I was in the Museum examining an array of stuffed arctic animals: moose, elk, beaver, wolf, wolverine, muskrat, bear and a whole spectrum of those animals whose pelts were the stock in trade of the Northcountry for generations. A sudden boom brought me out onto the street. In the clear blue sky above were the *Snow Birds*, Canada's elite flying corps. The planes had been flown in from their base at Moose Jaw in Saskatchewan to entertain and delight the partons of the Rendezvous with their skilful demonstration of figure flying and aeronautical gymnastics. Then as suddenly as they had appeared they were gone.

All too soon, my own departure time had also come. Emilio was waiting by the bus. Among the passengers was a gentleman who had, perhaps, one too many. Poking fun at me he asked, 'What would you get if you crossed an ice worm with a leprechaun?' And in answer I shot back, 'A-n-ice leprechaun, of course!' There was general laughter and he shut up. Meanwhile, on the undulating snowy landscape I watched a sledge and team of huskies taking a French Oblate priest on his missionary rounds. Soon all disappeared over the horizon and into a forest of jack pine. It was surreal. In the old days the indiginous population would flock to church three times a day while the missionary was in their midsts, but not any more. The forest dwellers seem to be getting the worst of Western civilisation and simultaneously losing the best of their own.

At Haines Junction I met Mr and Mrs Boyle from Ireland, he from Dublin, she from Belfast and a client of Clonard Monastery to boot. From the Junction a branch road leads to Dawson City, a settlement that had a population of 50,000 at the peak of the gold rush but was now reduced to a mere 350. The city is named after George M. Dawson, a diminutive hunchback who worked for the Canadian government as a geologist and Yukon explorer between 1873 and 1901. Dawson Creek, 'mile zero'at the southern terminus of the Alaska Highway, is also named after him.

Chief James Enoc of the Kluane

My memory of Destruction Bay is of a vociferous French-born ex-nun whose departure from the bus brought a palpable sense of relief to the remaining passengers. At Burwash Landing I had a quick word with Fr Huijbers, a Dutch Oblate responsible for several mountain mission churches, of which his lovely little log church at Burwash Landing was the chief. It was there too that I met Chief James Enoc of the Kluane. The discrepancy in height between us was verging on the ludicrous, but otherwise Chief James left me under no illusions: 'I'm the Chief,' he said, 'You can't go no higher than that.'

A Night in Beaver Creek

On our left as we departed Burwash Landing was the Kluane Game Sanctuary backed up by the spectacular St Elias Mountains. Emilio and I were the only passengers and thus it remained for hundreds of miles. Silver City wasn't the sparkling place that the title might suggest but then it, too, had its day in the sun. After skirting the southern shores of Kluane Lake – its 150 square miles making it the largest expanse of water in the Yukon – we covered interminable miles of mountain, snow and forest until a glow of light appeared on the horizon. It was Beaver Creek on the Yukon-Alaska border. As if inspired by one spirit we unanimously exclaimed, 'civilisation!' and indeed it was – but barely! The spot was too remote for television and our little transistor could pick up no sound at all from any part of the globe – Siberia, America, Europe, anywhere. We were fifteen hundred miles from the nearest major city and still five hundred miles from Fairbanks.

The motel was cosy and warm. A single room cost $10. Emilio and I signed up for a room with twin beds and paid out $6 apiece. Although our host assured us that supper was still being served, we meekly retired to sit on our beds and eat sandwiches. Emilio had taught me how to travel inexpensively. In a food-market he had bought two loaves of sliced bread, cheese, salami, pears, apples, chocolate and in case anything might be missing from his diet, he had a whole section of his travel bag filled with vitamins. I was learning. Dry sandwiches alone were not good enough. There was running water and a wash-basin in our room so we decided to have a drink. It was typical of his courtesy that Emilio left the only glass to me while he himself cupped up the water with both hands, saying with a broad smile, 'tea? bad for the nerves; coffee? bad for the nerves.'

One of the curious features of the motel was that there were no locks on the doors, neither inside nor outside. A notice warning of forest fires had a picture of Smokey the Bear on his knees, head reverently bowed, eyes cast down, paws joined. He was surrounded by other members of the animal kingdom all looking genuinely devout, prayerful, and anxious – foxes, wolves, skunks, deer, bear, squirrel. Even the wolverine beside him had put on a show of piety. Smokey had his head bandaged up and in the background was a burnt out tree. The caption read,

The community prayer of Smokey the Bear and his mates ...
'and please make people more careful.'

Morning came and we arose from our slumbers at day break. For breakfast we drank from the same tap as on the previous night and went on our way. It was 51 degrees Fahrenheit below freezing. Emilio was delighted: more stories for the grandchildren! Ken, the bus driver, told me that sometimes they get temperatures of 70 below. We passed a little west of Snag where a temperature of 84 below was recorded in 1948 – a record for North America. The Arctic forests through which we passed that day sheltered moose, lynx, wolf, fox, wolverine, otter, white ermine, wild mink, marten, red fox, squirrel, beaver, muskrat, cross fox, black gopher and dall sheep. The wolverine is a vicious little fellow. Smaller than a lynx, he is a great fighter, can give a bear a nasty time of it, and is strong enough to pull a quarter of a moose.

I cannot continue my story without reference to the Northern Lights or Aurora Borealis. As a child, in or about 1939, I remember my mother and sisters and myself going up on the ditch at the back of our house in order to observe this phenomenon. But never have I seen the Aurora Borealis so splendid as in the Yukon and Alaska:

> And the skies of night were alive with light,
> With a throbbing, thrilling, flame;
> Amber and rose and violet,
> Opal and gold it came.
> It swept the sky like a giant scythe,
> It quivered back to a wedge;
> Argently bright, it cleft the night
> With a wavy golden edge.[5]

Shortly after leaving Beaver Creek we crossed the frontier into Alaska, all 586,000 square miles of it, approximately eighteen times the size of Ireland. What caught my eye at the frontier was the number of abandoned cars, beautiful vehicles half buried in the snow. Ken said that many of them were confiscated or abandoned on foot of illegal trafficking in drugs. A hundred miles or so further on there was a man standing on the roadside waving a red flag. Ken stopped the bus and two Atabaskans, Paul Henry and Martha his squaw, boarded. Paul was a fur trapper. Having attended his trap run in the early morning he was going to relax at the local while Martha stocked up in household requirements. It was the kind of journey that any couple might make to the local village except that the village in this instance happened to be fifty-one miles away.

Tok Junction offers a choice: Dawson to the right, Anchorage to the left, Fairbanks straight ahead. We took the Anchorage road but only for a few hundred yards. Anchorage itself was several hundred miles south-west. There were a lot of groceries and alcoholic drink to be unloaded at Tok. Emilio and I gave Ken a hand at the task. A car engine had to be collected at a Texaco garage. It was resurrected from under a drift of snow where it lay in the company of a dozen or more skidoos and sledges.

---

5. Service, R., 'The Ballad of the Northern Lights' in *Songs of the High North*, p. 14.

Freeze to Death in Two Hours

The bus driver usually knew all the regular passengers by their first names. The harshness of the climate made one more conscious of being the neighbour's keeper. A car breakdown could mean freezing to death in two hours if help was not forthcoming. Even unattended petrol stations remained open all night with the polite request to 'take what you need and put the money in the letterbox'.

At Delta Junction, about a hundred miles short of Fairbanks, there was a public notice which read: 'Northern terminus of the "Alcan" Military Highway to Alaska.' I had difficulty in writing this because my biro froze. It was not only difficult to write at Delta Junction. It was also difficult to breath, and to see. Robert Service was right:

> If our eyes we'd close,
> then the lashes froze,
> till sometimes we couldn't see.[6]

In these conditions one had to be careful not to rush when alighting from a bus or leaving a house. The lungs might freeze and cause suffocation. For this reason we were advised to breathe through a scarf or cloth of some kind.

'North Pole' and Fairbanks

Some distance south of Fairbanks is a spot rejoicing in the name 'North Pole' and what else could one expect to see there if not Santa-Claus' House. And sure enough, there it was, standing among the tall snow-laden pines. It had its own post office and did a brisk trade, every correspondent receiving a reply from Santa himself. His address: Santa-Claus House, North Pole, Alaska, USA. That was in 1974. Word reached me some years later that the post office is no longer in service but this I can neither confirm nor deny.

We reached Fairbanks the second city of Alaska at four o'clock on the afternoon of 26 February. The city, which takes its name from an Indiana senator, began with a log cabin cache of

---

6. Service, R., 'The Cremation of Sam McGee', in *Songs of the Sourdough*, p. 65.

trade goods built in August 1901. By 1974 it had a population of about 20,000. We had a look about town, went to the tourist office, were awarded life-long membership in good standing of the Order of the Alaska Walrus, and given certificates to prove it. More treasure for Emilio's grandchildren! That night I stayed with the Jesuit community at the cathedral and had breakfast with them after morning Mass.

Walt Conant

It was now Ash Wednesday and, not forgetting the primary purpose of my presence in North America, I took the bus to Fairbanks University, the most northerly university in the Western Hemisphere. Walt Conant, the owner-driver of the university bus operated on an honour system. It was all very simple. He left a small tin box at the front of the bus with a note saying 'Fare: 50 cents each way'. You stepped aboard, paid your money, took your change if necessary, and waited for the driver to arrive at departure time.

Walt had a wonderful Santa-Claus-like appearance: red cheeks, red jacket, brown beret, leather trousers, suede boots and magnificent Karl-Marxian grey beard. Nor did he lack other Santa-clause qualities for he had a smile on his ruddy face and a courteous manner. This Fairbanks character had previously been in the wholesale business, had been a radio announcer, and was now running the university bus service. He made enough money to live on and was at peace with humankind.

Right inside the entrance door of the university museum was a stuffed beast, an eight foot tall Alaskan Brown Bear that once weighed 1,250 lbs – well over half a ton. Even in his stuffed condition, this kodiak looked positively magnificent. He represents the largest carnivorous mammal on earth. Among the other exhibits in the museum was a copper nugget weighing 5,200 lbs and a quartz crystal weighing 425 lbs. A moose that measured seven foot across the shoulders was impressive, but the Mammoth was in another category. For once I felt small and insignificant looking up at the monster that measured fourteen feet at the shoulders and sported seven-foot tusks.

Taco at Roberto's

Emilio and I were approaching the end of our time together. The mutual companionship had been a help in a strange land. Emilio had been speaking English for so long that he had a deep longing to use his native Spanish. Equally, he longed for a meal of Mexican taco. We tried without success to get taco in Sullivan's Hotel. Further inquiries revealed that within a mile or two there was a Mexican restaurant, run by Mexicans, serving Mexican food, and specialising in taco. The name of the establishment was Roberto's.

We trudged along through the snow and ice and I can assure the reader that it wasn't getting any easier. Eventually, flashing neon lights announced Roberto's. We had arrived. Emilio was delighted. He was scarcely inside the door when he was chatting away in Spanish against a background of Mexican music. Yes, they had taco, plenty of it, and for the first time in days, or maybe weeks, a thoroughly satisfying meal was served up to him. I don't remember what I ate at Roberto's but I do remember having the last laugh. During a brief conversation with the proprietor of this all-Mexican establishment I discovered that his father was from the west of Ireland and that his name was Roberto O'Higgins.

CHAPTER NINE

The Worker-Priest (1974)
'John-boy, the new kitchen porter'

If it took a long time to get to Alaska 'all de way by bus' it took even longer to get home. The research assignment that brought me to the North American was still far from complete. Yet, I felt that the journey into the arctic snows would always remain the highlight of the adventure and so indeed it did. It didn't take me long to conclude that my confrères back home were unlikely to sign up for courses in Fairbanks university. After a final upward glance at the magnificent eight foot Brown Bear, I thanked God that he wasn't alive and, bidding farewell to the city, continued on my way, first down the Alaska Highway, then by way of Williams Lake and Hope to Vancouver where I was met by my Irish confrère, Fr Brendan Boland, stationed in our monastery there.

It was at Hope that the snow had sufficiently melted to reveal the surface of the ground, something that disappeared weeks earlier between Fargo and Grand Forks in North Dakota. The driver was a little late leaving Vancouver but made up for it in entertainment. He assured us that while we were leaving Vancouver twenty minutes late we would arrive in Seattle twenty minutes early – which we did, as far as I can remember. Then he performed an extraordinary feat of memory. At the beginning of every bus journey the driver introduces himself, gives the departure and arrival times and the locations along the way or at the terminus where connections might be made for other destinations, e.g. 'This bus is leaving for such a place and will stop at X where you can get connections for Y and Z.' On this occasion our driver said that we would arrive at Seattle where there were connections for the following, naming every town and village all the way from Seattle to Miami, Florida; then listed connections for every town and village in the direction of San Diego and Mexico; and finally, named connections for every town and village between us and New York.

The most significant stop for me was Seattle and a long interview with a young Jesuit named John Topel SJ, and of this, more anon. A forty-six hour bus journey from San Francisco got me to San Antonio, Texas, just on time for St Patrick's Day and the centenary celebrations of St Patrick's Church. The chief celebrant of the Mass was Cardinal Manning of Los Angeles whom Archbishop Furey had invited to give the sermon. Manning was from Coolea in west Cork and a native Irish speaker so when the opportunity presented itself I greeted him as Gaeilge.

The further south I travelled in the USA, the more sparse and less attractive grew the theological pickings, the New Orleans Jesuit institute being a notable exception. But the journey into the south was not without its compensations and memorable moments. Just two weeks after leaving the low temperatures and the snows of Alaska, the oranges were falling off the trees along the streets of Phoenix, Arizona. And it was so good to feel warm again. While reading my breviary as I walked back and forth beside the bus a local man interrupted my orisons with the question, 'Are you a Bible-readin' maan?' Down south Bible reading was not simply an academic exercise; it was part of the daily spiritual diet of large numbers of ordinary citizens. And the further south I went the greater the interest was shown in that same book. Later in the journey and about two o'clock in the morning, I was making my way to a toilet in the back of the bus when I spotted a fellow passenger quietly reading his Bible. I gave him a nod of recognition and in reply he remarked, 'Good stuff there in John 2.'

As often as possible I sat towards the front of the bus. It gave the opportunity of observing the countryside but it also gave valuable opportunities of having a word with the driver or picking up a flavour of the local scene in snatches of conversation between regular passengers and drivers. The rule requiring drivers and passengers not to enter into conversation when the bus was moving was observed strictly enough for obvious reasons. Travelling through the night on roads that had yawning chasms to the right or left, there were times when an occasional word with the driver reassured me that he was wide awake.

One night between Baton Rouge and New Orleans I was chatting with a fellow passenger who told me that he was mar-

ried for twenty years and had four children. The remark precipitated the following exchange between driver and passenger:

Driver: 'You married twen'y years?'

Passenger: 'Yea.'

Driver: 'Same woman?'

Passenger: 'Yea.'

Driver: 'Me too.'

And with that the driver's right hand reached back for a cele-
bratory handshake. For years afterwards I often told that story
on parish missions, adding that when it comes to marriage in
Ireland we take such heroism for granted – the heroism that for
two whole decades a couple can continue to love one another
and at the same time forgive one another just for being different.
In more recent years that paragraph has either been deleted or
given as an example of the heroic. Ireland has travelled a long
road since the early spring of 1974. And so have I.

The significance of 1974

In 1974 I celebrated my thirty-eighth birthday. Although I was
unaware of it at the time, thirty-eight is considered by many
psychologists to be the beginning of a transition, a threshold
stage in a man's life, a bridge between early and middle adult-
hood, a time for review and reappraisal. During that year a
number of external events led to the making of significant decisions in relation to my life and work. I have written of one such
external factor in the foregoing chapter.

After all the travelling in North America in the spring of 1974
I resumed mission and retreat work in Esker. I also set about off-
loading some practices and activities that had become oppressive. School Retreats and Retreats to Religious went by the
board. So did the reading of newspapers and watching television, except perhaps for the 9.00 o'clock news on RTÉ. Did I become a hermit? No. There was always the radio, with its many
interesting programmes from Irish and foreign stations. Much
of the significance of 1974 flowed from the freedom that came in
the wake of these decisions.

In 1974 Irish Republicans were getting a particularly hard
time from all quarters. In September of that year I delivered the

annual oration at the grave of Liam Lynch. This was followed by an oration at the grave of Dick Barrett in December. Dick and three companions had been taken from their prison beds and executed as a government reprisal on the Feast of the Immaculate Conception, 1922. The following year I delivered the Sean Treacy commemorative oration and the next invitation to land on my desk requested me to deliver the oration at Kilmichael. This was the fourth such invitation in a short space of time and it was unlikely to be the last. I thought about it for a good while before declining. I wrote to the organising committee explaining that in my circumstances as a missioner, it would be inappropriate to continue on this very public political platform and the Kilmichael committee understood. After that, a rumour went about that I had been 'silenced' by my Redemptorist superiors. That rumour was without foundation. Whatever the faults of the Redemptorists, they are not given to silencing confrères.

School Retreats
School retreats were not high on my popularity rating, a view shared by many confrères, but there were notable exceptions. Some time during 1974, four of us were assigned to conduct a retreat for the girls in a large secondary school in a country town in Munster. For logistical reasons the school body was divided into four groups. That was fine. However, as there was a sizable group of disturbed and disruptive pupils in the school, the principal decided to divide them out evenly between the groups. Consequently, rather than having one disruptive group we had four. On the final afternoon of the retreat, and feeling worse for the wear, I bade a final farewell to that form of Redemptorist apostolate. Of the other missioners on this assignment two managed to survive without resigning from school retreats while a third, Fr Alphonsus (Fonsie) Doran, already well recognised as a survivor in chaos, had his reputation enhanced by the experience.

Nuns' Retreats
My work with Nuns began in Thomastown, Co Kilkenny. In 1965 Fr Geoffrey O'Connell and I gave a parish mission in the town and the Mercy Sisters in the local convent invited me to

conduct their Christmas Retreat. I agreed on condition that permission was granted by Fr Gerry Carroll, the rector of Mt St Alphonsus. I was a little under age – one had to be thirty years old – permission was granted, partly because there were so many requests for retreats that Christmas. The retreat went well. Nuns were known to take a motherly attitude towards beginners in this work and the Thomastown community was no exception.

By the early 1970s my experience of nuns' retreats was extensive. I had observed that through the late sixties and beyond, many of the sisters were being exposed to post-Vatican II theology and spirituality, but little seemed to be happening by way of change and development. Convent life was still held in thrall by debilitating structures. After much reflection I concluded that the missing dimension was experience. To fill this lacuna three of us designed a new kind of retreat. It would mean bringing the sisters out of their environment, out of convent routine, and into an ambiance conducive to rest, relaxation, reflection and growth. There would be good theological and spiritual input, more creative liturgy, open discussion and some home entertainment. Such an experience, we reckoned, would provide a powerful stimulus towards becoming more attuned to the spirit of Vatican II.

Three weeks was what I proposed for this experiment but my two confrères, Stan Mellett and Richard Tobin persuaded me that ten days might be more realistic; and so it was. The venue chosen was our Retreat House in the North Circular Road, Limerick. During the summer of 1973, two or three separate groups of Munster Mercy and Presentation Sisters made acts of faith in us, participated in the venture, and to the best of my knowledge, were well pleased. Years later, some of them at least, spoke of the experience as a major turning point in their lives.

Burning my Boats

Despite the success of the undertaking, it wasn't long until I came to the conclusion that there was no future for Religious Life, as we then knew it. Religious Life in itself was never an issue. It was the form in which we knew it. It seemed obvious to me that novitiates would be empty and that religious houses would be closing down. My undoing derived from the fact that I was naïve enough to say so. I told one novice mistress who at that time presided over three dozen young women in a regional novitiate, that the place would be empty in five years. That was the end of me. But, as things turned out, five years later, almost to the day, it was also the end of the novitiate.

For making such predictions there was a price to be paid. Hostility rooted in insecurity and disappointment surfaced. Nor were these emotions confined to members of Religious Orders. They affected the clerical world in general. Parish Priests no longer enjoyed the status of 'immoveable objects'. Hitherto their appointment meant a job for life. Curates who had spent their best years patiently waiting to inherit a parish now discovered that they were too old or that seniority no longer guaranteed promotion. Likewise, there were Religious Sisters who at times had felt the undue weight of authority and looked forward to a spell at the helm themselves; but in the turmoil of the day the opportunity sometimes slipped from their hands.

In the summer of 1974 three eight-day nuns' retreats were assigned to me. In view of my convictions about the future of Religious Life, the prospect of conducting three successive retreats to Sisters left me thoroughly uncomfortable. At the time I had a light motorbike, an old Honda 50 – I use the term old advisedly – and while in the vicinity of one of the convents situated in an exquisitely scenic areas of our country, I did a bit of reconnoitring. Talk of paradise! This was truly a heavenly spot. But to give a retreat there? That was another matter.

It was one thing to know that the structure of Religious Life was on the verge of collapse; it was something else to risk martyrdom for asserting the claim. In that frame of mind I returned to Esker and asked the rector, Seán Moore to excuse me from the retreats. He found replacements for the three assignments and with that I bade farewell indefinitely to Sisters' Retreats. I had burned my boats and there was no further employment for me through the long summer months until the autumn mission season began again.

Looking for a Job

For some time previously the concept of priest-workers was in the air and I had been deeply impressed by *Nazareth Diary*, Paul Gauthier's account of his experiences as a navvy in the Holy Land. I also knew that I was adaptable enough to work at more than priesting and preaching. I phoned Ned Myers, a brother of my confrère Fr Seán. Ned was widely known and respected not only in Killarney where he was Keeper of Muckross House Museum, but further afield as well. I asked him to have a look around and see if he could find me a job, any kind of a job, factory, hotel, tour guide, anything, provided I would be meeting people. He said he'd do what he could and that I could expect to hear from him again in a couple of days time. True to his word, Ned called me back to say that Mr Liam Kelly, manager of the Three Lakes Hotel would interview me any day of the coming week with a view to filling a vacancy for kitchen porter.

Interview

Mr Kelly and I agreed to meet for the interview on Thursday morning, 8 July. I packed my few belongings in Esker, went home to Kiskeam, and on the day appointed set off on my Honda. At the Three Lakes I self-consciously presented myself to the receptionist saying that I had an appointment with the manager. She explained that the manager was engaged but that he would be with me presently. With that, she invited me to take a seat, which I did. Satisfied that all was going well so far, I got up and walked about the foyer to get a closer look at some maps and pictures on display.

Before long I was shown into Mr Kelly's office and was greeted by a pleasant young man sitting at his desk. After a few introductory remarks I put my case for the job explaining that while on parish missions we work a lot with groups and I was interested in acquiring a better understanding of people in their work situations, et cetera and so forth. I could see that he was rather mystified by my utterances but willing to employ me provided the work was done. Liam Kelly was apologetic in telling me that the vacant post was that of kitchen porter. He also wondered how the staff might react to having a priest-worker in their midst, and if they should be informed in advance. I told him that as far as I was concerned, I'd prefer to break the news to them in my own way rather than make a big deal out of it and that I'd do it within the first couple of days. Mr Kelly agreed to my suggestion and we agreed also that the head chef – my immediate boss – would be an exception. He would be told that the new kitchen porter was in fact a priest.

When would work begin? As soon as I was ready. It was now Thursday. We agreed that I'd start on Saturday morning, 20 July 1974. Mr Kelly looked me up and down again and, choosing his words carefully, suggested that it would be well to come to work in casual clothes and waterproof shoes rather than dressing in my Sunday best. For those not familiar with hotel work, the office of kitchen porter is not the easiest job in the house. It places one in the way of getting both wet and dirty. I assured Liam that I'd come prepared. And forever I'll bear witness to the truth of the manager's advice about the clothes and shoes. Mr Kelly was not exaggerating.

Starting Work

The remainder of that day and the following one were spent at my home in Knockavorheen, Kiskeam. Saturday morning came. The Honda was loaded up with the army-surplus knapsack in which my worldly possessions were stored. I donned a fine pair of wellingtons that I had bought when appointed to Esker in 1972. Next came an old, but serviceable leather overcoat that had once belonged to a CIE man in Limerick, together with a pair of army officer's leather gloves that had fallen into my possession from God-knows-where. You see, I was not just facing hotel portering. I first had to negotiate the twenty miles across the bogs and wilderness of Sliabh Luachra to my place of employment.

On reaching the Three Lakes car park I secured the bike beneath the hotel and went in by the front door – for the last time of course. Liam Kelly was visibly pleased to see me in wellingtons and well he might be. I was really self-conscious as he led me through the dining room that was still half full of breakfast guests. We passed through the door marked 'Staff Only' and were presently in the bowels of the hotel, the kitchen. Liam introduced me to the staff as 'John O'Riordan, the new kitchen porter'. I smiled and shook hands all round and the manger left me in the care of Patrick, the head kitchen porter. Patrick was kind to me as indeed were all the staff as I was to learn little by little. It is customary in the south west of Ireland and particularly in Kerry to add 'boy' to first names and from the day of my arrival until the day I left Killarney I was simply known as *Johnboy the new kitchen porter.*

It was now ten o'clock and time for kitchen porters to be about the wash up after breakfast. Patrick Cronin, or Pat, as we knew him, introduced me to my duties. He showed me two large sinks, one for himself and one for me and bestowed on me what I looked on as my insignia of office, a pot scourer and scrubbing brush. The scrubbing brush was useful, the pot scourer indispensable. It was to be my inseparable companion and if it was lost for a moment, then so was I. There and then, we rolled up the sleeves and set to work. I washed and washed and washed and washed – cauldrons, frying pans, mixing bowls, mincers, spiders, fish-slices, whisks, ladles, sieves, trays of all descriptions, saucepans with handles and saucepans without, everything that could not go through the washing machine was pitched in my direction.

When I had washed more kitchen utensils than I had ever seen or scarcely knew to have existed, I was feeling truly sorry for myself, and my back ached. In order to check the time I straightened up, dried my hands and carefully pulled the watch out of an already saturated trousers pocket to see if the day was far spent. I'll never forget it: it was exactly 10.45 am. I had been working for three quarters of an hour. My respect for pot-scourers had already been established. To my new value system was now added the office of kitchen porters. From 10.45 am on that Saturday morning in July words cannot express the exalted status in which I hold them.

Lunch Break and After

At about 12.30 pm we took our lunch. There was a ritual here too. Each person was handed a tray and on foot of that, found for themselves a knife, fork, spoon and napkin. Next, on to the tray went the main course and a sweet, both handed out by the chef. I sheepishly took what I got and went down stairs to the staff room with my little tray. As I threw an eye over what others got for their dinner, it was obvious that I had missed out on a number of things but I kept my mind to myself. After a half hour or three quarters, I was back at the sinks again, washing, washing, washing, those endless pots and trays and whisks. Now, the chef had another job for me: to put a bucket of water in the stockpot or top up the *bain-marie*. Kiskeam had always been short on bain-maries, but on asking what it was, the chef showed me this useful piece of kitchen equipment for keeping food hot or simmering. The open tray was filled with hot water and standing in it were many tins containing soups, vegetables and other food mixtures.

If the wash up after breakfast was busy, it was nothing to the wash up after dinner. It seemed as if every cooking utensil west of the Rock of Cashel was being hurled in on top of me. Pat gave me a hand, and at this point I got an introduction to John, another kitchen porter. John was placid and kind. He worked away without a word, beyond an occasional comment on the weather.

By 3.30 in the afternoon the wash-up was finished. John and Pat told me that they would wash the kitchen floor that day but that I need not bother. It was a relief. There was more good news in store. Dermot, the head chef, strolled over to my scullery department and told me that I need not return at half past five but that I could have a half-day as I was only beginning. To this day, Dermot doesn't know what those words meant to me. He was an angel from heaven bringing me redemption and liberation from captivity, a breaker of chains. I was actually free for the rest of that day. To quote a Gilbert and Sullivan opera: 'Oh joy, O rapture! O rapture, O bliss!'

The Accommodation
The manager wanted to see me for a moment. I had not as yet been assigned my 'digs.' He told me to collect a pair of sheets, a pillow-slip and a towel, and go to a certain house about five minutes walk from the hotel where I would find a room. He assured me that as of now, there was a little single room vacant and that I might have it if I so wished. I don't know whether I got my little single room by accident or the goodness of the manager. Anyway it was mine. I picked up the bed linen and trotted along to the 'digs.'

The landlady was out. She worked in a shop nearby. Later, when admitting me to the house a big dog made an enthusiastic but unilateral declaration of friendship by jumping up on me. I did not reciprocate, somewhat to the annoyance of the owner. She assured me that he would do me no harm – they all do, don't they? Despite her assurances I keep well clear of the hairy monster. She inquired if I was Irish. I replied in the affirmative. 'You don't sound Irish,' she retorted. I didn't reply. As it happened, we did not have any further conversations during my stay except for a very occasional bidding of the time of day. She was English herself and must have suspected that I was not full-time in the hotel business.

Within minutes of getting the digs sorted out there was a Honda 50 zipping over Sliabh Luachra towards the county bounds with one happy kitchen porter astride. That night I fell into bed full of pains and muscular aches. For the next couple of days I wondered if my priest-worker career would come to a premature end. Gradually the physical adjustment phase passed.

All that first day I had kept my clerical identity a closely guarded secret. The staff were getting used to my presence just as they would to any other new recruit. They were all kind and helpful in initiating me into the different aspects of the work. According as I washed the various utensils I had to replace them in their proper department – the larder, the stillroom, the bakery, the scullery, and so on. Each part of the spacious kitchen had its own name and function. The pots went on a set of large shelves, the mincing machines and sieves and trays to the larder, the pastry piping to the bakery, the big steel mixing bowl was placed under the mixer together with the spade and whisk and spider. The cauldron went down stairs together with the roasting trays used for cooking red and white meat.

Gouldings Fertilizer

Next morning I was back on duty shortly before ten o'clock. (One of the benefits of being a kitchen porter is that one does not have to be at work too early in the morning.) A breakfast can be picked up at about 9.30 and one is ready for work before ten, earlier sometimes. On this second day it was evident to me that no matter how much care was taken at the sinks my trousers would be ruined in a couple of days and there was a good chance of developing more pains in the bones. Going down stairs to the toilet that morning I spotted a sack of cabbage. My problem was solved. I emptied the few heads of cabbage out of this fine strong plastic sack that had originally contained artificial manure. I borrowed a scissors from Cecilia or Alice – the pastry cooks – procured a piece of string elsewhere and in the twinkle of an eye I had tailored myself a brand new apron covering me from neck to toe. 'Brand' was the operative word, for when I wore this garment there was emblazoned across my chest the words Gouldings Fertilizer. Anyway that Gouldings sack was a real blessing and I not only wore it at work in the kitchen but also on the motorbike. It offered protection from both the rain and cold breeze that can be a scourge on the bike.

Being accepted in the kitchen proved so simple and easy that I decided on that second morning to start introducing my clerical self. The opportunity came at breakfast. Two of us were seated at the little sideboard in the staff room having our meal and making small talk. My colleague asked if I were full-time in the hotel business. 'No,' I replied, 'I'm a priest and a missioner, but as I haven't much work at this time of year, I took the opportunity of seeing how other people live.' To say that my companion was taken aback after that mouthful wouldn't do justice to the impact, but he bravely continued the conversation, minus the colour of an occasional expletive.

A little later, upstairs, as John and I washed up, I told him, too. These were my nearest fellow workers and I wanted them to be the first to know who I was in my regular life. I didn't tell anybody else that day but the two men to whom I had spoken passed on the word, as I had placed no embargo on their newfound information. After that I got one or other friendly 'arm on the shoulder' in case I was in difficulty or perhaps about to leave the priesthood. People were coming to terms with such matters in 1974.

Initiation Rites

Meanwhile, Mary another colleague of mine had her own way of making me feel at home. There was the matter of initiation into the community. With the knowledge of all the kitchen staff except myself, Mary came over and said, 'John-boy will 'ou go down?' 'Down where, Mary?' said I. 'Down in 'oor knees and kiss my … well not her hand anyway.' There was laughter all round and there it ended. All were happy that I had been caught out in this, my initiation ceremony, and that I had taken it all in good part. From that moment on, I enjoyed fully accredited status as a staff member of the Three Lakes Hotel.

The initiation rite was my real introduction to Mary, a girl whom I was to get to know as a good and generous young woman who provided the entire kitchen with much laughter and merriment by her open innocent ways. Mary had the precious gift of being able to tell people the truth about themselves without offence being given or taken.

Initiation complete, Cyril, the second chef, felt free to tell me of other initiation rites ranging from instructing a youth to collect mountain dew from the drip in the cold room to sending another unsuspecting victim down to the local greengrocer for fresh spaghetti, saying that the guests insisted on having it grown in Ireland and freshly picked from the garden.

Cyril was a red-haired, bearded Dubliner, volatile in temperament and in marked contrast to Dermot, the dark-haired phlegmatic Kerryman. Cyril kept up a running commentary on football, staff members, horses, life in general and the progress or lack of it in the preparation of the forthcoming meal. He was also a guitarist and singer who took a night job as entertainer in one or other local hostelry.

Tough Going for John-boy

After three or four days, enduring pains and aches and feeling sorry for myself began to slip down my anxiety scale. Maybe the entire undertaking was a disastrous mistake. Things were not as I had envisaged in terms of a fruitful apostolate through engaging people in serious discussion and debate on matters of religion. When coming to Killarney I had armed myself with a *Jerusalem Bible* and *Dutch Catechism*, the two hottest spiritual weapons of the day. Neither of them were best sellers nor matters of life and death among the hotel staff. In our kitchen there was time for little more than the few meteorological comments exchanged from time to time with John who rarely ventured further afield.

Time would reveal other dimensions to the duties of a kitchen porter: emptying garbage sacks and carrying buckets or tins of swill to the 'pigs barrel'. Anything that the pigs would not or could not eat went into William O'Brien's cylindrical garbage skip and was emptied twice a week. Unfortunately there were times when items such as detergents, broken glasses or other things not particularly conducive to animal health found their way into the 'pigs barrel' with disastrous consequences for the animals and financial losses for their owner, Pat-the-bar-man.

There were more cushy jobs in the hotel than emptying garbage: taking the eyes out of potatoes for example, a job demanding minimum output both physically and intellectually. An equally undemanding occupation was laying out eighteen trays of rashers and a similar amount of sausages.

'Are 'ou a priesht, John-boy?'

Having revealed my identity to Pat and John on the second morning, I added others to the list with a view to letting word spread. In no time at all, rumours were rife, not just about John-boy the new kitchen porter being six-foot-seven, but that he was a priest and a missioner. Some believed the accounts. For others it was too much. I went down to the staff hall for a meal and just arrived on time to overhear the washing-machine operator holding forth with his newfound information on John-boy. He was lecturing the attentive assembly, explaining to them, among other things, that the new kitchen porter was a Dominican priest. With that, I stepped up beside him and said, 'Sorry, I'm a Redemptorist missioner.' The poor man nearly went through the floor but quickly recovered his composure. Before joining the hotel staff he had been a knight of the roads and fond of the bottle, but now he was a sedentary member of the community and had not taken a drink for over four years. The man was fastidious about his appearance and his clothes always went to the cleaners, never to the laundry – 'more expensive but a better finish.' I could have learned a few lessons from him.

Following on this episode the entire staff were convinced in relation to my identity, with the inevitable one exception. 'Are 'ou a priesht John-boy?' she demanded. 'I am,' said I. 'Ou are a *dale!'* she retorted. I laughed. It was years since hearing the expression. It is a phrase meaning 'indeed you are not' but nurtured in a matrix of scorn and disbelief. After this altercation she spotted a medal hanging round my neck and grabbed hold of it crying gleefully, *'Now we'll see whether he is a priesht or not.'* She studied the medal carefully – a miraculous medal as it happened – and announced triumphantly *'Gor lads, he's a priesht alright!'* A miraculous medal indeed!

Satisfied as to my *bona fides* she wondered what kind of a priest I was because I certainly did not fit into any category she had heretofore encountered. She wondered if I said Mass, or if I celebrated Mass according to the general norms in the parish church: 'John-boy, do'ou say a full Mass or do'ou only say a bit of it?' Beneath a lot of this apparent frivolity there was something quite serious in which other staff members were also interested. Here was I, a priest, working as a kitchen porter and the concept of a priest occupying what was considered a menial position, even by hotel kitchen standards, was difficult to grasp. Another staff member who was anxious to have a full Sunday Mass checked with me if there would be Holy Communion at my celebration.

A Real Priest

One day during my stay in the Three Lakes a real priest visited our kitchen. He was a local curate and seemed to have some responsibility for hotel workers in town. The priest was organising a dance for his charges. In he came 'in full battle dress', immaculately clad, hair groomed, shoes shining, black from top to toe with the exception of the clerical collar which was whiter than white. There he was in marked contrast to everybody in the kitchen including myself. Even the manager, had be been present, might have felt a bit shabby in the circumstances. It was interesting for me to survey the scene and observe the dynamics from my sink in the corner.

At his entry into the kitchen the staff froze at once and were ever so polite and respectful as 'Father' moved about the kitchen giving us slips of paper with the relevant data on the forthcoming dance. He gave me one of the slips remarking as he did, 'You'll be there?' but not waiting for my response. It happened that I intended being in Kiskeam on that particular night and was genuinely sorry to miss the event. Then suddenly, he was gone, his departure as swift as his entry. And with his departure there came an audible sigh of relief as all turned to the scarecrow at the sink wearing his Gouldings Fertilizer designer apron and burst out laughing. There was a palpable sense of relief. But there was more. There was anger. What had gone wrong? He was working on behalf of the hotel staff, giving his time, but there was a dimension missing. It was a sense of slighted dignity, a perfunctory visit, somebody working *for* us but not *with* us.

Seeing a real priest in the round of his ministry interested me from other angles. As a missioner in the 1970s I often found myself in similar circumstances to the poor man in black that had just departed. In those days we missioners would visit hotels, factories, offices, pubs, every place where people worked or gathered, in order to publicise the parish mission. Having seen that real priest visit our kitchen, I concluded that it wasn't a ministry suited to everybody.

Food and food for thought

The food we received varied considerably. The breakfast was excellent but for me a bowl of porridge and a cup of tea was the limit. The porridge in the Three Lakes was nice. I took it every day. For those able for it there was much more available on the menu: fry, scramble, cereal, and toast. Porridge and scrambled eggs, as seen through the eyes of a kitchen porter, are abhorrent to a degree because it is difficult to clean the utensils in which these foods are prepared, particularly if they happen to get burnt. The supper was good, too, but the midday meal wasn't greatly to my liking.

For some peculiar reason which I could never fathom, cutlery was frequently in short supply. That's why I gradually reduced my layout of cutlery for all meals to one dessert spoon. It was invaluable, an all-round weapon that could be used for eating porridge, buttering bread, spreading jam, stirring tea, everything.

If the midday meal was weak, the instinct for self-preservation was strong. I kept an eye out for tasty pickings, a spud here, a scrap of freshly cooked meat there, a few Brussels sprouts or prunes or a bit of pastry. When Cyril was serving up dinners for the guests he might 'forget' to take a tasty morsel from the meat tray before pitching it in my direction. It is humiliating to think of it, but then, humility is a much-needed virtue if a kitchen porter is to maintain equilibrium and self-esteem. I often thought of humility while in the hotel, particularly when I went down stairs to the car park to pray. I would walk up and down reading my breviary. From time to time I'd salute guests coming and going but they would generally pass by without a word or nod of recognition. I thought of how different it might have been had I stood there in clerical garb rather than in wellingtons and a Gouldings Fertilizer sack. In those days the priest was at the top of the social ladder, a position from which many envious social climbers would have gladly toppled him.

The Work Rota
The work rota involved what is called a 'straight day' and a 'split day'. Though technically there was no time difference between a 'straight day' and a 'split day,' in practice there was a tremendous difference. A straight day seemed to me like a half-day, whereas a split day was like a day and a half. In a split day, the normal pattern was to work from about 9.30 in the morning to 3.00 o'clock in the afternoon and again from 5.30 pm to 9.00 pm or later, allowing for a meal break. Staff members had a day and a half off in the seven-day week. We enjoyed good flexibility in relation to that day and a half. One option was to take the day and a half as a unit, usually an afternoon plus the entire following day. Another was to save up one's time off by making a private agreement with a fellow worker and take three days or a week when one had saved that much. As long as the work was done no questions were asked.

It was interesting to observe the dynamics of the staff as nine o'clock approached each evening. Naturally enough, people were anxious to get off at nine and all going well that would happen. However, if guests arrived in shortly before nine ordering such things as steak, chips and mushrooms, they were liable to have colourful imprecations relating to sex and travel showered upon them, or be branded as fornicators of unparalleled prowess. When the rest of the staff had finished, the kitchen porters had to scrub the kitchen floor. My colleagues were more than kind in this regard and I usually emptied some garbage cans instead, or just wound up work for the day.

Early in my employment I had to seek a minor adjustment to the schedule but it posed no problem. I had been billed to give a lecture on Holy Wells and Patterns to the Duhallow Folk School on 25 July. On that evening in Cullen, Co Cork, I led the traditional 'Rounds' at St Latiaran's Well and afterwards delivered the lecture at 8.30 o'clock in the community hall. There was an impressive turn out at the lecture. The invitation to speak had come from the late Fr Seán McSweeney, a man who always gave me a warm welcome to his community. I felt his death quite a lot. *Ar dheis Dé go raibh a anam uasal.*

Getting to Know Killarney

Initially, on a split day, I'd go straight to bed for an hour in the afternoon and then celebrate Mass somewhere. With the passage of time and growing fitness, the afternoon siesta was occasionally abandoned in favour of exploratory trips about Killarney and its hinterland.

There was a staff member named Mary working in the still-room. She was a girl of sparkling personality, a native of Cork city and currently attending university there. I used to refer to her jokingly as Mary-the-pots because she had all the teapots in the hotel in her remit. Mary had never been on a motorbike. I said to her one day, 'Mary I'm going to Torc Waterfall on the Honda; would you like to accompany me?' She availed of the opportunity and even on a bike as weak as a Honda 50, she experienced some of the exhilaration that is the privilege of bikers on a pleasant summer's day. We toured the grounds of Muckross House and drove to Mangerton car park, Torc Waterfall, Ladies View and Moll's Gap. The Honda loudly grumbled its way up the hills, but being the bike that it was, it never let us down. And what we lost in time on the climb we made up in the return. A mild acceleration set us on a free flight for home.

It was during my work in Killarney too, that I first explored the Gap of Dunloe. On another split day I took the Killorglin road and branched off for the Gap. The road was relatively quiet until Kate Kearney's Cottage came into view. From there to the Gap was like a fair. With so many horses and riders I thought I was back again at Cahiramee. As horse riding was nothing new to me, I declined all the urging to go through the Gap on a mount. Instead, I strolled leisurely along the dirt road, enjoying not only the scenery but the reaction and excitement of tourists, many of whom were viewing the world for the first time from the back of a horse.

Fuller Integration

After finding my feet at work and getting over the initial muscular pains and tiredness, I participated more fully in the life of the hotel community, and went along with them to one or other of the singing pubs. The Laurels had a reputation for providing good entertainment but The Jug of Punch was our favourite, because Cyril, our chef, and his assistant, Mike, provided the music there. From time to time, when our entertainers needed a break, they would call upon us for a song, with the result that more than once I found myself at the microphone in the Jug of Punch.

There was no hard drinking among our staff. For one thing pay packets didn't allow of it. At that time wages were low. My own take-home pay amounted to about twenty-three euro, but many of my work mates were on much less for our forty-five-hour week. We just came to the pub for a bit of relaxation and to get away for an hour or two from the grind of the work place. Variety or excitement at work usually came in the form of extra work, a wedding party perhaps, or a bus tour. I enjoyed hearing a regular appeal, 'John-boy, have 'oo the brish?' The caller and I shared responsibility for keeping the kitchen floor swept, and we also shared a close relationship to the spoken Irish. Though sounding quaint in the English tongue, she demonstrated a perfect use of both broad and slender vowels as used in Irish.

One Mass

During my stay in Killarney I had only one opportunity of celebrating Mass in the hotel. Sunday after Sunday the staff would ask for it but, sadly, I always had to answer 'No'. The local church authority did not allow of it on the grounds that the place for fulfilling the Sunday 'obligation' was the parish church. There was a privilege in Ireland since Penal times that allowed the Sunday 'obligation' to be fulfilled by attending Mass anywhere. I didn't inform the reverend gentleman nor argue the point. After all, my mission in Killarney was to wash pots and pans and not instruct the local clergy. However, the priest in question decided that I could celebrate Mass in the hotel on the Holy Day, 15 August, on the grounds that it might facilitate the staff. Little did he know that every day is the same in the hotel, Sunday, Monday, Holy Day and holiday. Again, I bit my lip and refrained from offering information on the running of hotels. Once the permission for Mass on the Holy Day was granted, I asked no more questions.

Finally, the day came when I had permission to celebrate my one and only Mass with my colleagues in the hotel. It was a very simple affair, no procession, no singing, nothing, but the effect on the little congregation of management, staff and the few guests that joined us was stunning. We had planned on having music and song but Cyril, our chef-cum-musician slept in and we had to proceed without his liturgical services. One person present hadn't been to Mass or sacraments for some considerable time. She turned to her friend and confided that she was so happy to be there. A couple of days later she went to the Friary to celebrate the Sacrament of Reconciliation.

At this Mass it seemed appropriate to dispense with that venerable liturgical act known as 'the collection'. Later, I was both touched and embarrassed to discover that my work colleagues had done a whip around and presented me with ten pounds, a lot of money in our circumstances and the equivalent of two weeks' wages for the young man who operated the washing machine. As well as affecting the hotel staff, the effect on the visitors must have been pretty good, too, because one of them walked up to me at the end and handed me another ten-pound note. No wonder I was embarrassed; the two gifts amounted to more than my week's wages.

Two Revelations

Having worked for some weeks in the hotel I had begun to think that the entire venture was a futile exercise. At worst it was doing somebody else out of a job. These were my thoughts until one afternoon when the manager was passing through the kitchen. I was sweeping the floor and keeping an eye to twenty-four chickens that I had put cooking in the oven – I was bold enough now to give the chef a break. The manager stopped and we exchanged a few pleasantries but then he got serious. He told me that my presence in the hotel was having a profound effect on the entire staff and not just those in the kitchen. He said that it was making all the staff, and particularly the younger element, take a new look at their own values, their understanding of priests, and indeed, their understanding of themselves and of the hard work of service in which they engage day by day. On a lighter note, he said that his own staff was boasting among other hotel staffs in town that they had a priest in the family. And I'm sure glad to have acquired so many good and gentle brothers and sisters of mine.

Ten days after my work in The Three Lakes had ended, I was back in town on some other business and called in to visit my old colleagues. I thought that by this time they might have forgotten, but they hadn't. There was so much excitement in the kitchen that the manager had to come in and get us to tone down as we were impacting on the dining room guests.

May God's blessing envelop all at the Three Lakes who shared with me that summer of '74. They have ever been in my prayers and Mass and I hope that their lives have turned out well in the intervening years. Ever since we worked together I have had a special *grá* for hotel workers everywhere and a particularly high regard for kitchen porters.

It was on the night of revisiting the hotel that I got the ultimate confirmation of my priest-worker venture. Up in The Jug of Punch two lovely girls put their arms around me and said, 'John-boy, you're a great ould fella. You came down among us.' My eyes filled with tears.

CHAPTER TEN

An Educational Revamp (1975-1977)
'To live is to change'

After all my globe-trotting and priest-working in the spring and summer of 1974, it was back to work on parish missions which was my official work for almost all of my Redemptorist life. Between then and the Summer of 1975 my mission schedule included such places as Athlone, Co Westmeath, Strokestown, Co Roscommon, Kilconiron, Co Galway and Bodyke, Co Clare. There is a touch of nostalgia in remembering the Bodyke mission as this chapter will unfold.

The Redemptorist provincial administration of the time encouraged further education and re-education. Much of that impetus came from foreign mission influences particularly from the Philippines. Fr Steve Mahony, the vice-provincial of the Philippine Mission, had almost made it mandatory for confrères to up-date their theology and pastoral strategies. At home the influence of Fr Seán O'Riordan can scarcely be exaggerated. His breath of vision, compelling lectures, engaging personality and sheer goodness reached everybody in the province. Despite his many commitments in Rome and elsewhere, he never lost contact with the confrères in the home province. Seán always found time to up-date us on the latest happenings in Rome and in a generous and unassuming fashion share the benefits of his spiritual and theological riches.

The significant sermon seminar held in Esker in the early 1970s also had a wide and positive influence on the quality, style and content of preaching in the province. Many of the brethren contributed but the really inspirational material came from Fr Dick Tobin. Dick has a genius not only for composing vibrant prayer formulae but also for digesting abstruse theology and making it pastorally intelligible. Both of these gifts contributed much to the overall air of satisfaction with the seminar.

Myers-Brigs Workshop

Now that both school retreats and nuns' retreats were off my personal agenda, my summers were free. I was in a position to avail of that further education encouraged by the provincial administration. My appetite was whetted during my North American research assignment. On my return journey I spent a week with the Redemptorists in Spanish Harlem in New York and from that stay there were two specific memories. The one was that of meeting and conversing in the monastery with a Puerto Rican gangster who, in his own words, was 'becoming a bit churchy'. He told me of his muggings, his robberies of lead from the Edison Company's electrical instalments – 'You get a truck load of lead and you're a wealthy man'; and of how he and his gang could strip down a car (i.e. take the four wheels off) in twenty five seconds – 'I timed it myself.' The more important and beneficial memory is of my first encounter with the Myers-Brigs Type Indicator, a Jungian-based and relatively simple psychological system for arriving at some appreciation of one's own and others' personalities. It so happened that during my stay a fellow Redemptorist was conducting a Myers-Brigs workshop with a view to setting up a pastoral council. He invited me to participate in the workshop and so I did.

On reading the results of my test, the instructor told me that I was a 'classic wheel spinner'. Well, I thought it was nice to be a classic something, but what did 'wheel-spinner' mean. It means that I had all the distinguishing characteristics – introvert, extravert, thinker, feeler, sensate and intuitive – developed to more or less the same level, with 'extravert' and 'thinker' leading by a short head. This newfound information had a practical significance. It indicated a personality type that needed a good deal of variety. He said that if I was left in the same job and in the same place for too long, performance would suffer. Experience had already taught me that, but here was a psychological basis for it.

A later exploration of the Enneagram 'to get a number for the jersey' as my confrère Fr Peter Mulrooney used to say jokingly, also proved beneficial. Answering 'yes' to eighteen out of twenty questions confirmed that I was a number eight. And that news too, had a ring of truth about it. It was Peter Byrne that first introduced me to number eights. Telling me that he was one himself, Peter went on to say that the animal symbol associated with a number eight is the rhinoceros. But in the enneagram there is a distinction made between the raw rhino, so to speak, and the redeemed one. The distinction between the two as Peter graphically described to me is that when the raw rhinoceros comes up against a stone wall he goes through it, whereas the redeemed one jumps over it. It is said that women normally prefer to have a number other than eight on the jersey; but where would the world be without gender balance even among rhinos?

Discovering SUMORE

While researching the various institutions of learning across the USA and Canada the name SUMORE was popping up repeatedly. Good things were being spoken of it across the land. Consequently, even before getting there, I had it short-listed as a potential place for personal studies.

This mysterious place called SUMORE turned out to be at Seattle University, a well-respected institution of learning established and run by the Jesuits. I spoke to John Topel, SUMORE's engaging and energetic young director. He explained the philosophy on which the programme was based, and as he did I thought to myself, this is the kind of programme we had been attempting to devise for the nuns at the Limerick Retreat House. Here it was fully developed and operational at Seattle University Graduate School under the title, *Seattle University Master of Religious Education*, or SUMORE for short. The programme was designed to suit people interested in personal development and the promotion of a religious education geared to the post-Vatican II world. Then and there, I made up my mind that should the opportunity come my way for study, SUMORE would be my first choice.

That opportunity came sooner than I had expected and by the spring of 1975 I had signed up for the master's programme to be completed in three summers, provided I had turned in a satisfactory thesis and synthesis. (The synthesis was a kind of comprehensive examination that focused on personal growth and the gaining of insight rather than merely on academic performance).

In preparation for the first university term there was some required and recommended background reading. I can remember joyfully and enthusiastically engaging in that reading during a mission in Bodyke and Toomgreaney. It was the month of May. The weather was glorious and the work wasn't overly absorbing. During the sunny afternoons I'd walk outside the presbytery, listening to the larks and reading Carl Roger's *Person to Person* and *Memories, Dreams & Reflections*. I can never look at those books without a certain nostalgic yearning for the SUMORE days.

Flight costs to Seattle on conventional carriers seemed prohibitive and all my plans might have disintegrated had it not been for the efficiency of John Topel or his secretary or both. A letter arrived from the secretary informing me that Laker Airways, a low cost carrier, flew from London-Gatwick to Vancouver for £144 return. And even though Freddie Laker never got beyond primary school, he was in no small way responsible for my master's degree at SUMORE. I am eternally grateful to him for that because I have derived endless pleasure and a lot of personal and pastoral benefit from the Seattle experience.

A Bold Experiment at Seattle U

The SUMORE programme started in 1969. The initial student body was largely if not totally comprised of priests and Religious between the ages of twenty-five and forty-five. At the end of the 1960s Catholic church life was in ferment and the folklore of the early days of SUMORE is that 'everybody married everybody else'. Priests, nuns and brothers were meeting away from their communities in a congenial atmosphere and there was the almost inevitable pairing off, which in many instances led to marriage and sometimes, sadly but inevitably in the circumstances, to wounded feelings.

By the time of my arrival on the scene on 8 June 1975, SUMORE had opened its doors to some lay students, not all of whom were Catholic. It had also successfully weathered the above mentioned growing pains while the seeds of decline had not yet been sown. In fact, SUMORE was at its peak. I'm not saying that there was no romance, but most of us managed to get through three summers without change of status or home address.

The SUMORE experience was holistic – a new word for me at the time. There was a fine balance between the various branches of psychology and theology.

Taking the degree over a three-year period allowed time to absorb the content of the summer residential courses and catch up on required reading. The number of core courses was deliberately limited in order to foster an interactive developmental atmosphere among the student community. Students were allowed take some electives, but they too were limited, and for the same reason.

We all lived in Bellarmine Hall on campus. There was single room accommodation unless otherwise requested. We participated in creative liturgies, had organised and informal group outings and shared dining facilities with the professorial staff. Other factors that enhanced community building were visits to Goldies on Monday nights for half-price beer or classes in American Folk Dance and Swedish massage.

Finally, SUMORE operated a self-assessment system in examinations. One can understand how this latter was a continual bone of contention with the university administration and may ultimately have been responsible for the demise of the programme. Nevertheless, SUMORE maintained a good academic standard without losing sight of the primary vision, the success of which ultimately rested on the development and transformation of persons.

Good Memories

It was a wonderful blessing to find myself in the right place at the right time. If ever the reality surpassed the dream in my life it was at SUMORE. There was a splendid professorial staff, including, Dr Thomas A. Francoeur from McGill University in Montreal, Dr Andre Auw from Carl Roger's Centre for the Study of the Person in La Jolla, California, Dr Stanley Marrow SJ, a scripture professor from Babylon, Dr Nancy Kehoe from the East Coast, Dr Henri de Lavalette from Paris, Dr David Standil Rast from Vienna, Dr Anthony Padovano, still fresh from his studies in Europe, and Dr Larry Carlin and his wife Kay, who jointly taught the Communications Psychology course, and as an optional extra, Larry taught Swedish Massage as well.

Larry also invited me to apply for a Fellowship at Carl Roger's Centre for the Study of the Person in La Jolla where he himself lectured. He promised his own support and assured me of support from other staff members if I expressed interest. It was a tempting offer and I didn't turn it down lightly. However, taking it up would have involved a significant career change, and having considered all angles I decided to remain a traditional Redemptorist missioner though with more psychological and spiritual background than when first coming to study at Seattle U.

The entire experience of SUMORE came at a good time in my own life. The grounding in developmental and communications psychology and in conflict resolution was of inestimable personal benefit and helped me to live more comfortably with myself. I grew in confidence and in the ability to be more relaxed, open, and less judgemental.

At the end of the final term each had to present a synthesis, that is, a personal reflection, showing how we had integrated the various component elements of the SUMORE programme into our lives, and how we thought this had benefited us as persons and how it might enhance our future ministry. The presentation, made before at least two staff members, could be in written or oral form, although one of my classmates did it through mime. My own synthesis was a written submission followed by an oral hearing.

Researching Irish Spirituality

For a thesis I chose the area of Irish Catholic Spirituality. At the beginning of the second summer, when Dr Anthony Padovano was lecturing on the influence of American Puritan culture on American Catholicism, it suddenly dawned on me that there was a parallel dynamic operating back home in Ireland. From the mid 17th century Anglo-Saxon Puritan culture had come to envelop the entire English-speaking world. This cultural envelopment was true for Catholic Ireland throughout the 19th century because our own Irish language was in steep decline. It was only while researching Irish Spirituality that I became aware of a rising interest in 'Celtic Spirituality,' of which Irish Catholic Spirituality is the richest expression.

As a part of a research strategy I drew up a list of twenty people whom I planned to consult on what they considered integral to the Irish traditional approach to God – people such as Seán Ó Riordan, CSSR (theologian), Seán Ó Ríordáin (file), Seán Ó Duinn, OSB (Celtic Scholar), Seán Ó Faoileáin (writer), Brendan Kennelly (poet), Diarmuid Ó Laoghaire SJ (Gaeilgeóir), Margaret McCurtain OP (historian), Cearbhúil Ó Dalaigh (judge). Seán Ó Ríordáin, file, died before I had the opportunity to hear him. So did Cearbhúil Ó Dalaigh. Seán Ó Fáoileáin was not very well but talked with me on the phone. My contact with Brendan Kennelly was also by phone and it was the most fascinating twenty minutes I ever spent on the phone with anybody. Others contacted were generous with their time and rich in their insightful contributions and to them all I am much indebted. When the thesis was finally presented before the end of the third summer in Seattle, it was well received by staff and students alike.

Jim Bodeen

The student body that had assembled in mid June 1975 was highly rated by the staff. Many of us were priests or religious but by that date there was also a growing number both from among the laity and from other Christian traditions. One of these, Jim Bodeen by name and a Lutheran by tradition, became my best friend at the university. Although 40 years old, I had not as yet made any social contacts outside of the Catholic community. Jim was a poet, teacher, philosopher, married man and as I write, a well respected publisher in his native Yakima, Washington State. With him at Seattle were his wife Karen and their three young children. Living in a Catholic atmosphere on campus was as big a culture shock for them as coming from Ireland was for myself.

Jim and I were kindred spirits. We spent many hours together and had a benign approach towards each other's eccentricities. Shortly before we parted in August 1977 he composed a poem entitled *After 40 years, Living with a Lutheran*. As far as I can recollect he pushed it under my door at a time when tears would not have been far from either of us:

Eight days from now
You'll be gone.
I'm trying to forget
Already. Today I ran away

Five miles. John
You make one
Want to be
Priest.

You don't think there's anything wrong
In being mad.
I'd walk with you.

CHAPTER ELEVEN

Reducing Dreams to Reality (1977-1990)
Two adult education projects

The educational revamp in Seattle, combined with seven years of seminary training in the fields of theology, psychology and spirituality, provided me with a good background for lecturing and seminar work in these fields of learning. It was providential that on my return to Ireland after the summer of 1976 a request had come in to the monastery at Mt St Alphonsus for a priest who was willing to work with a group of adults in the area of Christian Development. This was exactly the kind of work for which I was being newly prepared. I gladly undertook to fulfil that particular request but without relinquishing my regular mission work. That was never in question. The adult work that I had envisaged was to be conducted in the 'off season' between late November and Lent. It would be complimentary to mission work and preferably conducted where I had already given a mission.

Fás – Growth in Christ

The request for somebody to conduct an Adult Development programme had come from Mary Carr, a primary school teacher living in Newcastlewest with her Donegal-born husband, Eamon and their young family. The request was the catalyst that spurred me to sit down and devise a course that I named *Fás – Growth in Christ*, or simply *Fás*. Unfortunately I didn't protect the title legally and the term was later applied to a new government employment scheme. *Fás* (Growth) as I envisaged it was a Christian developmental programme for adults, a growth into Christ.

Conscious of the Celtic penchant for the sprint over the long haul, *Fás* was organised on the basis of six two-and-a-half hour sessions within a fortnight. Saturday Vigil Mass had not yet been introduced so that the programme ran on Monday,

Wednesday and Friday, or Tuesday, Thursday and Saturday of two consecutive weeks. With intervals of a year there were options for a second, third, fourth or even fifth module if so desired. Nor was it required of participants to have done the first module in order to be eligible for the second or subsequent ones.

The structure also allowed for running *Fás* in two adjoining parishes within the same time frame. Consequently participants who missed a night in their own parish could make it up on the following night in the next. Sessions started at 7.30 pm. The first hour was devoted to theology. It was followed by a tea break and that was followed by a communications psychology seminar. The final minutes of the evening were spent listening to a little classical music, during which members of the group were invited to relax, rest, pray, or just *be*.

The theological input and discussions aimed at deepening knowledge and understanding of the Christian message. The communications seminars were calculated to foster personal development, group cohesion and leadership. In the 1970s people were not used to participation in such programmes and were relatively show to engage in theological discussion. However, they enjoyed the communications sessions from the word go and the relaxed atmosphere generated at them quickly led to vigorous participation in theological discussion.

Launch in Newcastlewest

Initially the thought of undertaking a *Fás* programme posed a personal threat. Up to this point in my life, preaching was my medium. Lecturing was an entirely new experience. It meant standing before an audience who could talk back. It was my custom to put a lot of study and effort into preparing sermons. The same effort went into the preparations for lecturing. Still, I was nervous. Mary Carr had guaranteed that the people would be there. That much was certain but it didn't minimise my other catastrophic anxieties: 'Will it be a disaster?' 'Will I be able for the questions?' 'Will I make a fool of myself?' These fears were not permitted to occupy centre stage but they were all there lurking in the wings. Nevertheless, it was with high hopes that I set out for Newcastlewest on 17 January 1977.

After that first evening my doubts were consigned to oblivion. The group had reacted favourably and indeed, enthusiastically. Over the next fifteen years, then, in conjunction with mission work, I conducted these programmes in many centres throughout Ireland, among them Ballybunion, Nenagh, Limerick, Carlow, Bagenalstown, Listowel, Loughrea, Ballinasloe, Stranorlar, Kinvara and Dundalk. In all, over 2,000 people participated. During those years several groups took more than one module with a maximum five. They were:

1. A New Step for Adults
2. Sacramentality and Sacraments
3. An Introduction to Sacred Scripture with a focus on Luke-Acts
4. Ministry and the People of God
5. Mid-Life Development

In the event of meeting individuals on parish missions who sought more than we could offer from the pulpit, I'd suggest to them that they might organise a *Fás* programme by setting up a small committee, recruiting about fifty people (in the hope that forty might turn up), finding a suitable venue with facilities for a cup of tea, and getting the blessing of the parish priest. This invitation separated the talkers from the doers and led to new talents surfacing among those who took up the challenge.

Since any kind of adult development group tends to be mostly female, I stressed the need for gender balance in the recruiting process and to some extent at least it was achieved. A unique situation arose in Nenagh where after the usual mixed programme an all-male one followed by popular demand. With the passage of time it became evident both to the participants and to myself that I was totally at home in this kind of work. I loved it, and still do.

This period of my apostolic life holds many treasured memories of growth and blossoming on the part of the students. Two mildly entertaining ones come to mind: one arose out of the psychology seminar and the other from the theology. A well-settled couple from the rural hinterland of Ballybunion attended the programme and wholeheartedly entered into the spirit of it. On one occasion the psychological topic exercised the wife so much that she woke up her husband in the middle of the night asking, 'Johnny, do you think that I'm a simple or a complex personality?'

On theological matters, there were people in Muine Bheag, Co Carlow, talking across the garden fences until two o'clock in the morning, hotly debating the merits of high and low Christology; and that at a time when Ireland's energies seemed to be totally absorbed in the contraception debate.

The *Fás* programmes were innovative and successful but I always felt the need to include another dimension, namely, an element of physical exercise calculated to refresh the mind and body once or twice during the evening sessions. This finally happened at the end of my involvement in the programmes. While based in Dundalk, we had a secretary in the monastery, Nuala Begley by name, who in the middle to late 1990s was contemplating a career change. To that end she trained to degree status in the area of counselling and psychotherapy as well as enhancing her skills by adding diplomas in such things as massage and health and fitness issues.

Aware of each other's gifts and training, Nuala and I decided to work as a team in the conduct of a weekend for adults in Mt Oliver Pastoral Centre near Dundalk. I lectured on some theological material; we shared the psychological input; and as well as giving instructions on health and fitness Nuala charmed the participants by the manner in which she involved them in lighthearted physical exercises that refreshed and rejoiced everybody in the hall. To me that weekend was the ultimate in my years of adult education, and sadly, for a variety of reasons, not least of which was a transfer back to Munster, it was also the last such programme we conducted together.

Paris Interlude
The opening up of Redemptorist life in the post-Vatican II world presented many fine opportunities for those willing to take them. The best poised to seize them were the missioners because their work was seasonal and we had few or no institutions to be maintained. Consequently, our mission staff began to find alternative summer employment in Britain or North America or avail of study opportunities.

In 1978 after the successful beginning of my career in adult education, I determined to invest new energy in acquiring some facility in French. In the Juvenate my standard in the language had never progressed beyond failed Intermediate. However, through his daily stories about France, our teacher, Fr Fred Dunne, filled our young hearts with a romantic longing to visit that country. So enthusiastic were we that Michael Heagney, Frank Tobin and myself made up our minds to cycle to Lourdes. While our enthusiasm couldn't be faulted we three budding Francophiles had neither money nor French. In later years Michael and Frank were appointed to the Philippines and had to grapple with new languages there. At home in Ireland my enthusiasm for French stood the test of the years and even in my early forties I attempted to make up some ground on the language as you shall presently discover.

True, I had been to Paris previously and hobbled along linguistically with my *cupla focal* or *petit peu* because I love the way in which the French do liturgy. At the Communauté Monastique de Jerusalem in St Gervais I find the music and chant more conducive to prayer than in most places of my acquaintance. Equally wonderful is the Liturgy of St John Chrysostom in the Russian Orthodox Cathedral of St Alexander Nevsky in the same city. Here one can hear one of the world's most famous choirs on an average Sunday morning. But don't expect to see a spectacle, a performance so to speak. I couldn't locate the choir on my first visit but its effect on me was profound. On my second or third visit I searched for the source of this heavenly choir that sent my spirit soaring to the heavens only to discover in a rather obscure corner a small group endowed with angel voices.

Prior to telling you of attempts to improve my French, there is one other liturgical experience that will always stay with me. It was Holy Week. Fr Vincent Kavanagh and I decided to go to Notre Dame de Paris for the solemn Mass of Chrism. The cathedral was crowded to capacity when we arrived and, not being sure whether or not we would be allowed participate as concelebrants, we only half-heartedly edged our way in the direction of the sacristy. On the way we admired the layout of the church for the evening's liturgy. A series of tables covered with white cloths and seasonal flowers formed an extended altar from the sanctuary to the front door. All seating arrangements were in choir-formation so that the entire congregation could face this long beautifully appointed 'altar'. We had also observed that priests has been going up towards the altar rails and being allowed through to the sacristy but by the time we got near, all access had been closed off.

The liturgy was about to commence and the hundreds of priests were already beginning to file down either side of the above-mentioned altar. A good lady, obviously with some authority about the place, approached us and asked if we would like to concelebrate. We nodded affirmatively and with that she led us into the sacristy, hurriedly decked us out in appropriate vestments and said *'suive moi'*. We did follow her and, leading us by a circuitous and unobtrusive route, she landed us into two vacant stalls amid the Canons of Notre Dame. Being a historian I was intrigued at finding myself among this august body whose predecessors had been at the centre of much attention in the lead up to the Revolution in 1789.

The chief celebrant of the Mass was the able and popular Cardinal Jean-Marie Lustiger, the Paris-born son of a Jewish couple from Poland. At the sign of peace, he engaged us in a few words concerning our Irish identity and membership of the Congregation of the Most Holy Redeemer. That personal word with Lustiger was a special moment for me. The Mass ended with the sound of the full-throated congregation, the two choirs, and the two organs harmoniously proclaiming *Magnificat anima mea Domino* in the glorious *tone Royale*. It was as if everything that is and was and is to come was truly magnifying the Lord.

All that is by way of background to the summer of 1978 when I took an intensive language course in L'Institute Catholique de Paris in the hope of gaining an insight into a world outside of the Anglo-Saxon culture. My hope of mastering French was not realised but at the end of a month I got a pass in the beginners' course, the first time I ever gained such a distinction in *la langue française*. Madame le professeur had no illusions about my capabilities nor did she hide the fact from me. I wondered was she another number eight. She would say things like, 'Ah pere Jean, you are very bad. But you are old (forty-two!). It is not easy to learn when you are old.' Or again, 'Your pronunciation is very gooth, but *votre écriture, oh! Formidable*.' Had I enough French I'd have invited her to join my communications psychology courses in *Fás*. A little more affirmation might have helped. Back to Ireland I came clutching my *satis bene* and thereafter continued to deteriorate in understanding the language of culture and gentility.

The School of Personal and Pastoral Development

The success of *Fás* encouraged me to take a more daring step and in the winter of 1979 I devised the School of Personal and Pastoral Development (SPPD), a residential summer school in Cluain Mhuire, Galway. It functioned from the summer of 1980 until 1987 when a decision was taken to sell Cluain Mhuire

The patrons of the school were Dr Joseph Cassidy, Bishop of Clonfert and later Archbishop of Tuam, and the Provincial superior of the Irish Redemptorists. Among those willing to serve on a consultative board were Archbishop Cassidy, Dr Margaret McCurtain OP, Department of Modern Irish History NUI Dublin, Alice O'Sullivan, Kerry Diocesan Council for the Family, Dr Gearoid MacEoin, Professor of Old Irish and Celtic Studies, NUI Galway and Fr Harry Bohan, Founder/Director of Rural Housing & Rural Resources, Shannon. To all of these I am indebted for lending the weight of their names and goodwill in the cause of human and Christian development.

Running the SPPD was difficult work. Some of my confrères thought it foolhardy but wished me well. After all, it didn't seem to make much sense for a lone missioner without a house or a car or a staff to set out on such a venture. Pearse's words kept ringing in my ears:

O wise men, riddle me this:
What if the dream comes true?[1]

I had stepped beyond the conventional limits and either the 'wise men' or myself would be proven right. That made me all the more determined to reduce the dream to reality.

Recruiting students was nerve-racking. After trying every form of advertising within my power, from talking to Donncha Ó Dúlaing on Radio Éireann to the use of posters and circulars, to cajoling friends and acquaintances, I managed to muster twenty adults who arrived in Cluain Mhuire on 6 July 1980, committed to stay for one month. Four children, the offspring of two couples on the course, together with four lecturers, made up the full compliment.

Recruiting the teaching staff was easier. In that process I had only one major setback and in the long run that proved to be a

1. Pearse, P. H., 'The Fool' in *The 1916 Poets* by Desmond Ryan, p. 21.

blessing. Larry and Kay Carlin from the USA had to cancel at short notice. Not knowing anybody else who could teach the kind of Communications Psychology course that I had in mind, I decided to teach it myself. And while teaching it to a satisfactory standard, I derived a great deal of personal benefit as well. Dr Tom Francoeur of McGill University, Montreal, taught developmental psychology; Ms Maura Hyland took catechetics; and Fr Martin Drennan of Maynooth and now Bishop of Galway taught a scripture course on Luke-Acts. Other professorial staff engaged over the years included Dr Patrick Hannon (Maynooth), Sr Mairead Hurley (Killeshandra), Máire Ní Dhuibhir (New Inn), John Moriarty (Moyvane) and confrères Seán Ó Canainn (Rome), Leonard Martin (Brazil), Con Casey (Dublin), Richard Tobin (Esker) and Brendan McConvery (Dublin).

Innovations

The above-mentioned personnel presented the core courses in theology and psychology. To these were added some recreationally orientated elements that fostered personal growth and community building at a practical level. A priest introducing massage to an adult group on a Religious Education Programme in the Ireland of 1980 strains the imagination. Yet, when the students had checked and rechecked that it wasn't a joke, most participated enthusiastically in learning the basics of this new skill.

Folk Dance was less threatening. Helen McCarthy, herself a student, was the inspiration for the folk dance workshops and physical exercises. I had come to know Helen and her husband Dr Dan when they attended a *Fás* programme in Limerick in 1979. Together with their two youngest children, Andrew and Ailsa, they signed up for the SPPD and proved faithful and resourceful allies. The following year Helen became a staff member and so remained. She and Alice O'Sullivan from Ballybunion were refined trouble-shooting artists, whose skills were in frequent demand by the number eight.

Group outings, too, were an integral feature in the overall learning process. It was on the outings that a lot of the best developmental work was done. My role was that of historical and archaeological guide, but I was aware of a whole other interpersonal dynamic operating in the relaxed atmosphere of these excursions. As we toured the Burren, Connemara, Cong, Clonmacnoise, Clonfert and the Aran Islands, all the course-work was discussed, parsed, analysed and applied. The family run Beach Hotel in Salthill was a regular venue for such appraisal and analysis. The Beach (sadly, no longer a hotel) was our 'local' and it had the added advantage of having music and a dance floor. Whenever I feel nostalgic for those days in Galway it is The Beach that comes to mind.

After the 1980 experience, the staff and students urged that the riches of the SPPD be opened up to people who for one reason or another could not afford to spend four weeks away from home or work. After that, there were courses specifically tailored to catering for a residential week or even a long weekend. This proved satisfactory, not only in terms of more people deriving benefit from the school but also in getting the school on a even keel financially. In all, during its existence, the School of Personal and Pastoral Development touched the lives of between seven hundred and a thousand people drawn from twenty nine counties in Ireland together with a scattering from England, Scotland, France, Germany, South Africa and the USA.

In terms of finance, the SPPD broke even, apart from the first summer, when there was a deficit of six hundred pounds. As I set out on the project that summer, John O'Donnell, the provincial superior in 1980, kindly told me that if I had a financial deficit to let him know, and that he'd cover it from provincial funds. And true to his word, John did.

CHAPTER TWELVE

New Horizons From Dundalk (1990-2003)
A small wee taste of the North

In the Snows of Montreal
By the mid 1980s I was overdue a sabbatical and, having discussed the matter with my friend and mentor, Dr Tom
Francoeur, we agreed that I'd read for a PhD under his personal
supervision at the Educational Department in McGill University
in Montreal. I was getting close to fifty years of age and the pursuit of the degree would refresh and renew me for what remained of my mission career. All necessary documentation was
duly submitted and I flew from Shannon on 6 January 1985.

Major disappointment was in store for me at McGill. The
ground rules had been changed in the educational department
and we were not permitted to proceed as planned. By this time I
had paid the fees for a half year and while it is one thing to pay
fees in, it is more problematic to get them out. Rather than return
to Ireland, then, I opted for the theology department and signed
up for a PhD in church history. The subjects I took – Patristics,
Reformation Theology and Newman and the Oxford Movement
– were interesting in themselves, and I benefited from the discipline of studying and writing papers at doctoral level. But something more pastorally useful was what I had hoped for.
Therefore, when the term concluded at the end of April I
switched over to the Education Department to pursue some excellent courses in Mid-life Development and aspects of
Psychotherapy and Psychiatry. At the end of these studies I collected my fifteen credits and returned to mission work in
Ireland. Ah! But it was lovely to get home to Ireland that June,
because in winter, Montreal is cold, cold, cold, and for much of
the time it caused my poor head to split with migraine.

During the late 1980s the edge had gone off what used to be
described as 'The New Mission'. The high energy levels abroad
in the 1960s and most of the following decade had dropped considerably in the country at large, and this was reflected in our

missions. We were older too, and missioners were not at all as confident in attempting to 'convert the world' as we had been during the previous decade. Perhaps we had garnered a modicum of wisdom along the way and most were happy to settle for giving solid missions. These solid missions would not ruffle feathers among either priests or people nor did they challenge them to venture beyond the security of the tried and true. Having said that, these missions had their own good effect and for many people they were a lifesaver in terms of giving the customary boost to regular parish life.

Carrickmacross Mission

In the summer of 1990, Fr Raphael Gallagher, the provincial, asked me to join the mission team in St Joseph's Monastery, Dundalk, and that I did on 27 August of the same year. Up to this I had done very little work in North Leinster and the Six Counties, just a couple of novenas and no mission. For my first assignment, Fr Kevin Browne, the rector of St Joseph's, asked me to lead a mission in Carrickmacross. Mgr Connolly was willing to accept my strategy for such an undertaking. The plans included full house-to-house visitation by the missioners. They also envisaged house meetings; these latter to be conducted by lay parishioners themselves. And furthermore the leader of each meeting was detailed to report back to an open assembly of priests and people in the community hall at the weekend. In preparation for chairing the house meetings, I gave the volunteers one or two sessions of basic training.

The most memorable aspect of the mission was the weekend assembly. As each leader stood up to report, it became evident that the Catholic Church in Carrickmacross was rich, and more than rich, in personal resources. It had an abundance of dedicated men and women, competent speakers, solid in the faith, and in no way blind either to the strengths or weaknesses of the church and community in Carrick. Since their role was to 'report' they felt comfortable in telling things as they were, without fear or favour, without complaining or carrying chips on their shoulders. The entire event was an inspiration and it crossed my mind more than once that the parish was blessed with an extraordinary fund of talent and good will on which to build.

Working North of the Border

Working out of Dundalk furnished ample opportunity for experiencing mission work north of the border. Crossing the border was always a bit of an ordeal and no matter how satisfactory things went during the mission there was always a sense of relief on returning to the South. Missions in the North were easier, the response more enthusiastic. The Catholic community held their religious leaders close to the heart, and the priests for their part were spoilt compared with their counterparts south of the border. On the other hand the clergy tended to be more conservative in theology and pastoral practice.

The Troubles

The Troubles, as the thirty years war in the North was euphemistically described, were partly responsible for the close relationship between priest and people. During the Troubles both Catholic and Protestant communities felt under threat and among the Catholics at least, the people found security in their religious tradition symbolised by the presence of the priest. But the closeness of the bond is rooted further back, namely in the Plantation of Ulster in the early 17th century.

Everyone up North has a story to tell concerning the Troubles. My own story is brief. During parish missions, especially in border areas, I was aware that the British forces conducted a fairly steady low-level harassment of the people that was rarely reported in the news media. During a mission this might take the form of holding up parishioners at the border so that they would be late for Mass or Mission Services. Helicopter activities, especially the heavy military helicopters, were often in the air in the vicinity of the church when services were afoot, notably during the Crossmaglen Mission in February 1999.

In another parish in South Armagh, when I arrived for the 7.00 am mission Mass I found that the front door of the church had been kicked in during the previous night. The local people were unanimous in their opinion that the vandalism was the work of the military and that the strategy was to interrupt the mission. To report the incident immediately would have led to cordoning off the church and the cancellation of the mission service. Based on that view, the local people did not report the incident until after the ten o'clock Mass when cordoning off the church for a few hours was unlikely to interfere with the mission.

Being a southerner, my knowledge of the bigotry in the North was a matter of hearsay. However, one telling personal example happened to me during a mission in Lisnaskea, Co Fermanagh. While staying at the priest's house, I went out each day to do my work in the parish. There was a man whom I regularly met on the road and naturally enough, in a small country place, I would salute him but he never acknowledged it. Towards the end of the mission I met him in the middle of the day when he was engaged in cutting a hedge by his house. I saluted him as usual and he stuck out his tongue at me. I found it hard to believe such behaviour from a man of about fifty years of age but that's the North, some of it anyway.

Looking at the soldiers on duty at checkpoints, one could not help seeing many of them as little boys armed to the teeth. They had the misfortune to be in the army and find themselves assigned to 'a tour of duty in the North'. They were not supposed to hold ordinary conversation with the public. However, they did not always abide by the letter of the law. From talking to one of these men it was obvious to me that he might as well be in the remotest part of the world. And maybe as far as he was concerned, he was. At a checkpoint about one o'clock in the morning I had a few words with another one of these youngsters. He was eighteen and had to do a thirty-six-hour continuous stint. No wonder that mistakes were made at times. The army had some thoroughgoing blackguards and sociopaths in its ranks, too, and some of their activities do not bear description, but thank God I did not have to witness their barbarity.

Towards the Ceasefire

It was during my years in Dundalk that peace came to this troubled part of the country. A lot of exploratory contacts were made around the Dundalk area, a number of them within the monastery. Our phone was bugged, so was our phone in Belfast and even in Limerick. In Dundalk monastery there was one particular phone limited to local calls. I picked it up to call a friend in town one night but accidentally hit the wrong buttons.

Instead of the friendly 'Hello' a voice said in a strong English accent 'Her Majesty's Service'.

Even during the worst of the war there was some behind-the-scenes talking and my confrère Fr Alex Reid was usually in the thick of it, although in day-to-day conversation he would give the impression that his sole interest in life was the Dublin Minors – hurling of course. Then came serious talks of a ceasefire. My room in the monastery was on the second floor. It was a standard size room but at the end of the same corridor was a somewhat larger room that had various uses. I was not supposed to know who my neighbours on that corridor were at certain times, and the truth is that I didn't. However, other more observant monks discreetly informed me that at various times they had seen John Hume or Gerry Adams or Martin Mansergh or some other high profile figure going up the back stairs to that room. Dinners too were sent up to these guests.

Knowing what was in progress on my corridor I had some apprehension lest the monastery itself be bombed. But that passed and little by little a feeling of expectancy filled the air. We prayed and we hoped, and finally the first ceasefire was announced. There was quiet jubilation, if such there can be. On the next mission over the border the new atmosphere was palpable. There were setbacks at both political and military levels but at last peace seemed to be bedding in.

During my time in Dundalk I contacted the Irish Commission for Prisoners Overseas offering to write the odd letter to whatever prisoners might be assigned to me. I was given the names of two young female Republican prisoners and corresponded with them until their ultimate release under the Good Friday Agreement. Through my contact with the two young women assigned to me, a third lady who was serving a fifteen-year sentence in jail for killing her husband, started writing also. Over the years I came to know something of the English prison system and prison names such as Old Elvet, Styal, Wormwoodscrubs, Maghaberry, became part of my inner vocabulary.

It was painful to read of the daily humiliations to which the two Republican prisoners were subjected. From whatever information was available to me it seemed that the two were found guilty by association, rather than having done anything seriously wrong. But in the climate of the time they were given a thirty-year sentence and had served more than half of it before political developments brought them relief. At an early stage of their sentence it seemed evident that the prison authorities were determined to break their spirit. The two, therefore, made a mutual pact that they would not allow this to happen. After many years in English jails, things began to improve on the political front and they were transferred back to Maghaberry prison in Northern Ireland. I visited one of them there; the other had just been released as far as I can recall. Some years later, in 2007, there was footage of the newly elected deputies for the Northern Ireland Assembly on their way into Stormont to take their seats. And who was among them in all her beauty and elegance representing her constituency but one of my two friends. It is a moment that I will always treasure.

Scotland – My 'Outside Farm'

Although some work in Scotland came my way over the years it expanded considerably after my transfer to Dundalk. The expansion was not consequent on the transfer but having my base in Dundalk brought Scotland considerably closer to me than heretofore. A parish mission in Girvan in the late 1970s was followed in the mid 1980s by a series of Solemn Novenas in honour of the Mother of Perpetual Help in St Margaret's, Johnston and St John's in Barrhead, both in the diocese of Paisley in Renfrewshire. The novenas involved a team of Redemptorists from the London province with whom I worked on these occasions.

After several wonderful Novenas this work came to a sudden end on a rather sour note. In a sermon to a packed church and in the presence of the bishop and many of his chapter, my reflections on *bidin' together* and the complexity of human and marital relationships today did not go down well on the sanctuary. Consequently, the next Solemn Novena scheduled for Paisley Cathedral was cancelled within a couple of hours or less.

Getting the chop in Paisley diocese on that occasion has never been a matter for boasting but neither is it one for repenting. It was no misjudgement on my part but a carefully calculated strategy that I well knew might result in expulsion. From the very first Solemn Novena in the country it was evident that many good people were burdened with guilt while at the same time having little or no chance of escape from church legalism, civil bureaucracy and personal and family commitments. They had become resigned to the apparent hopelessness of their 'sinful' situation. In the circumstances it was difficult to close one's eyes to these people and the gospel imperative to bring good news to the poor. Getting short shrift in Paisley diocese was a small price to pay for going out on a limb and bringing good news. The only regret I had was that some of my confrères were deprived of a couple of weeks' employment.

Besides novenas there were other things that attracted me to North Britain and the Scottish Isles. My interest in matters Celtic took me to Old Melrose where St Cuthbert dedicated his young life to God, to Lindisfarne of St Aidan, to Whithorn of St Ninian, to Lismore of St Moluag, Iona of St Colmcille and the beautiful Applecross of St Maelrua. The approach to the Applecross peninsula I shall never forget and I feel compelled to share with every reader my feelings on that occasion. Here is what I wrote about it in *A Pilgrim in Celtic Scotland*:

My companions and I made our pilgrim approach from Inverness via the low-key loveliness of Strath Bran. Taking a left turn at Kinlochewe, we drove at our usual leisurely pace skirting Glendocherty on the left. Before reaching Torridon village, I thought my heart and mind would burst in an attempt to absorb the extraordinary natural beauty that was opening up with every twist and turn of the road. Rarely have I seen anything so entrancing. There was something about the texture of the light, first on the mountains, then on the lake – Upper Loch Torridon, which, under the influence of the evening sunshine, presented itself as a golden mirror. As if the general scene were not overwhelming enough, there were, too, the haunting underwater reflections which left me – not without pain, it must be said – at the edge of finitude, because the beauty of the scene could neither be adequately contained nor expressed.

We stopped by a little church and ancient graveyard,

which in far off times some Celtic monk may well have designated 'the place of his resurrection'. And then, continuing to feast our eyes on the unfolding scene, motored on. By the time we reached Shieldaig, driving proved impossible once more; the scene called for pause and silent contemplation. So there we sat on the edge of Loch Shieldaig, with Loch Torridon beyond, and beyond that the waters of the North Minch and beyond that again the Isle of Lewis, and beyond that everything that the Celtic imagination is capable of creating, even to *Tír na nÓg* and heaven itself.[1]

Caution: God at Work!

It was on the very next day or the day following of that holiday-cum-pilgrimage in 1987 that the real opening up of Scotland came though a providential error. I filled up the petrol tank at a garage in Fortwilliam and drove the short distance to the parochial house where we asked for and got some altar breads for Mass. On resuming our journey the car refused to start. It still refused to start despite the efforts of a local mechanic. We were faced with spending the night in Fortwilliam. That was easier said than done. It was high season and every B&B had 'no vacancy' signs. It would have been a matter of sleeping rough were it not for the kindness of Fr John Archie McNeil, the parish priest who had already given us the altar breads. In the morning the car was towed to the garage and by lunchtime the problem had been identified. A mechanic had finally got a kick out of the engine and smelt diesel. Our car ran on petrol. I had filled it with diesel. Before leaving we thanked John Archie and I assured him that if ever he needed temporary help or replacement I'd be happy to oblige if the occasion presented itself.

The following Lent John Archie needed somebody to replace him for two weeks in Fortwilliam. In the next parish, that of Corpach and Caol, there was a young parish priest named Roddy Wright who befriended me and would call in from time to time to see if all was well. And at times all would not be well. An attempt to cook peas resulted in a saucepan full of the

1. Ó Ríordáin, John J., *A Pilgrim in Celtic Scotland*, Columba Press (Dublin), 1997, p. 84.

proverbial bullets. Another attempt, this time to cook in the microwave, ended up in smoke. Fortunately it was not more serious. Seeing the microwave on fire I pulled the plug, opened the windows and said my prayers. After that my diet was extremely simple until such time as Roddy turned up and cooked me a good meal.

Soon afterwards Roddy was appointed Bishop of Argyll and the Isles. I wrote to him and said I'd be willing to work on parish missions in his diocese if any priests were interested. He circularised his priests to this effect. A chain of missions on the mainland and islands ensued: first the Outer Hebridean Island parishes of Eriskay, Bornish in South Uist, Benbecula and North Uist, Castlebay and Northbay in Barra; then Campbeltown in Kintyre and the inner Hebridean Island of Islay. Missions outside of Argyll and the Isles included work in the dioceses of Dunkeld, Edinburgh and Aberdeen including a mission in the Orkney Islands in 1996. I had been looking forward to that mission in Orkney as it would furnish me with ample opportunity for chatting with the Orcadian writer, George Mackay Brown, whom I had first met in 1987. My plans once again validated Robert Burn's insight,

The best laid schemes o' mice and men
Gang aft a-gley,
An' lea'e us nought but grief an' pain,
For promis'd joy![2]

When I arrived at Kirkwall in June 1996 people were still talking about George's funeral Mass in Kirkwall Cathedral.

Sara Dreever, the parish clerk in Kirkwall's Catholic church, told me that her mother had been George's personal secretary and had prepared his manuscript material for publication. On a special shelf in her home were copies of his many writings – over forty works of prose, plays and poetry.

Of all the parishes in which I worked that of Dingwall was the most far-flung. It spread from 'sea to shining sea' – the Atlantic to the North Sea in this instance. There were three weekend Masses, all on the Sunday, because Vigil Masses had not been introduced at the time. These involved a round trip of

---

2. Burns, Robert, 'To a Mouse' in *Poems*, Penguin Edition, 1983, p. 89

160 miles. Some sixty miles from Dingwall was the second church of the parish. It was an old bakery that had been neatly converted into a church in 1988 and was a *bijou* in its own right. Because of my presence in the parish Ullapool enjoyed its own Holy Week ceremonies, and that for the first time. Almost everybody in the congregation was involved as our total compliment at any service was under twenty. The pause for breath by the singer of the *Exultet* was more pronounced than usual, because she was eight months pregnant.

Donegal fishermen enjoyed a high reputation in this little West Highland village, not only because of the considerable amount of money they contributed to the building fund of the little church but also the shining example these fine young men gave in coming ashore and parading up to church for Sunday Mass. Although many other trawlers from Catholic nations in Eastern Europe and elsewhere availed of the shelter and safe anchorage in Lough Broom, inspiration came to the locals from the Donegal boys.

Craig Lodge Family House of Prayer

During my early days in Argyll Bishop Roddy made occasional references to Craig Lodge, a new house of prayer that had been set up near the West Highland village of Dalmally. He was open-minded about the venture and ready to give it a chance. When Lauri Hanratty of the Family of God Community in Dundalk was embarking on a pilgrimage to Iona, I suggested that he call at Craig Lodge to see what the place was like. He not only came back with a good report but also with a letter from the management inviting me to conduct some retreats on Celtic Spirituality at the lodge. Ever since I have been back and forth to Craig, preaching, lecturing, and staying over when accompanying pilgrim groups to Iona and elsewhere.

The founders of the House of Prayer are Calum and Mary-Anne MacFarlane-Barrow who went on pilgrimage to Medjugorje in the early 1980s and were so inspired by it that after a lot of prayer and reflection they turned over their lives, their home and their family business to setting up a house of prayer in October 1988.

Craig Lodge Family House of Prayer is a sort of ongoing miracle in the West Highlands and that is particularly due to the fact that it is a house of prayer if ever there was such. The Holy Eucharist, the Divine Office, adoration, meditation and the rosary are foundational to the prayer-life and, understandably in view of its origins, devotion to Our Lady of Medjugorje is deeply cherished.

From the beginning the apostolic outreach from Craig Lodge has been consistent and impressive, particularly in the area of feeding, clothing and housing the poor in Eastern Europe and Africa. Through the inspiration and organisation emanating from the lodge, massive quantities of goods are regularly shipped abroad and community members drive trucks laden with supplies across the Continent to former Yugoslavia, Romania and elsewhere.

Early on in their venture of faith Calum and Mary-Anne established the Krizevac community, a name derived from the Slavic word for 'Cross'. It caters for young adults who commit themselves to spend a substantial amount of time living in community, a year perhaps. Under the guidance of Mary-Anne these young men and women follow a rule of life involving work, prayer and spiritual formation. Initially Mary-Anne and Calum had hoped that the Krizevac community would produce vocations to the priesthood and religious life, and it did produce some. What it produced in far greater abundance was vocations to the married state. For ex-Krizevac members who choose to marry, Craig Lodge remains a sort of *alma mater* to which they return as often as possible to celebrate the Sunday Eucharist with the community. That contact is enriching not only for the couples but also for their children. In consequence what was once a deChristianised area of the West Highlands now has many committed Catholic families.

Shortage of Priests

It was in Scotland that I first encountered parishes without curates and then parishes without priests, and now churches being closed down. On my most recent assignment there I spoke to a priest with responsibility for three parishes, together with other priestly responsibilities. And the situation is deteriorating with every passing year, not only in Scotland but in many parts of the

Catholic world. It wasn't my awareness of the shortage of priests but the personal encounter with the man of the three parishes that focused by attention on the question of where the future lies. Increasing the burdens on willing shoulders is hardly satisfactory. My three-parish friend has not yet reached middle age but he is already worse for the wear.

We pray for vocations – that's good. But it may well be that the Holy Spirit will lead us to solve our present difficulties in ways that the church as an institutioin is not yet ready to contemplate. If the current restrictions on priesthood continue many 'hungry sheep' will be denied the nourishment of the Eucharist. It is hard for some of us to see this as the wish of the Good Shepherd. Perhaps it is time to open our minds to the possibility of married priests and women priests. Not that such moves would be a panacea for all ills, as the experience of other Christian churches makes clear.

Ecumenical Progress

The Ecumenical dimension of my life developed slowly. There was no Protestant in our area of Duhallow and it was only towards the end of my primary education in Kiskeam that I first saw a Protestant whom I knew to be such. He was a garda stationed in Ballydesmond who occasionally cycled past Kiskeam School and if his passing happened to coinside with our lunch break we would lean over the retaining wall to get a glimpse of him. That ended my ecumenical experience for another three decades until Jim Bodeen and myself developed a rich friendship at Seattle University. After we parted in 1977 almost two decades more would elapse before any further developments in the ecumenical field.

During the summer of 1991 I spent two weeks on the island of Iona. The second week was by way of holiday but for the first week I attended a seminar on Celtic Spirituality conducted by the abbey warden and his wife, Philip and Alison Newell. The couple noted my contributions to the discussions and invited me to lecture there for a week the following year, 1995. During that week my audience was mostly drawn from the Protestant tradition, including Presbyterian, Anglican, Baptist, Lutheran. Here, for a few summer days we united in sharing a common humanity, a common decency, a common Early Christian and mediaeval heritage and communal prayer before our beloved Lord and God. Is there more to ecumenism? Perhaps. Let me not deny the eternal quest for the fullness of Truth.

Since then I have been ecumenically involved with many groups, notably in Belfast, Bangor and particularly, Rostrevor, Co Down. Through this ecumenical work I have come to know and greatly admire Ken Newell, the 2004 moderator of the Presbyterian Church in Ireland. Ken invited me to come to his church and deliver a lecture on 'St Patrick and the Scriptures' to the Clonard-Fitzroy Fellowship in the adjoining hall. Not only were there believers from the four main churches but from many others besides – Baptists, Salvation Army, Society of Friends, Brethren, packed into the hall. There was a wonderful sense of unity that night. With Patrick we were fellow believers in the Risen Lord Jesus. We celebrated Patrick's phenomenal knowledge and appreciation of the holy scriptures. Ultimately, what probably made everybody happy and relaxed, I think, was the fact that Patrick had never mentioned either Rome or Justification by Faith.

Rostrevor has become my ecumenical base-camp. Canon Dermot Jameson of the Church of Ireland invited me to give a lecture on Celtic Spirituality at St Bronach's School of Celtic Christian Studies in Rostrevor. The lecture went well and the next time Dermot wrote to me, my name was at the bottom of the page among the 'Directors of the School'. That was news to me and provided no small amount of merriment. The fact that he hadn't asked my permission or consent told a lot about our easy happy relationship. We were kindred spirits and could comfortably dispense with some formalities.

St Bronach's School is more in the realm of the mind than in terms of concrete blocks. In view of its geographical location its 'student' population, all adults, is mostly drawn from the north-eastern counties, especially Down and Armagh. We meet for a number of study days throughout the year and spend a few days together at the end of April or early May. These group outings have brought us on pilgrimage to historic and holy places in the West of Ireland, to the Aran Islands, too, and further afield to follow the footsteps of St Columbanus on the Continent and to explore the Northumbrian world of St Bede's monastery at Jarrow, St Aidan's on the tidal island of Lindisfarne, St Hilda's famed establishment at Whitby, and as I write, the plans for a pilgrimage to Oberammergau in 2010 are well advanced.

The combination of prayer, liturgy, history and good fellowship on these pilgrimages has cemented solid bonds of friendship within St Bronach's. Having lectured on the historical background to the English church and the Synod of Whitby, I composed a little jingle to the air of 'Monto' in order to liven up a rather lengthy coach journey and summarise the who's who and what's what at the Synod held there in AD 664.

One of the principal goals of that synod was to settle a long-running controversy about the dating of Easter. With the passing of the centuries Rome had updated its system for calculating the date of Easter but the Christians in the remote islands of Britain and Ireland had continued to follow the old Roman system which had been brought by early missionaries. This in practice often meant a gap of some weeks between the followers of the new Roman system and the old. Tempers were running high in the 7th century and when St Hilda offered to host the synod in 664 the protagonists of both sides were there in strength – King Oswy and his queen, the gentle Irish Bishop Coleman of Lindisfarne, the Gaulish missionary Bishop Agilbert and his arrogant spokesman Wilfrid of Rippon. The synod was a rather stormy affair.

I went up to Whitby, Whitby, Whitby.
I went up to Whitby to learn more
And see where Abbess Hilda, Hilda, Hilda,
Hosted a great Synod in 6-6-4.

She invited Bishop Coleman, Agilbert and Wilfrid,
King Oswy and Queen Eanfled to afternoon tea.
So they all went up to Whitby, Whitby, Whitby
They all went up to Whitby on the sea.

They discussed the rite of baptism, tonsure and Easter
And sparks they went aflying, as you shall see
For Wilfrid lost his temper; just why, I can't remember,
And Coleman with a whimper said he could not see

The need for uniformity, the stress on mere conformity –
The kind of thing demanded by the Holy See.
So they stormed out of Whitby, Whitby, Whitby
And let Hilda do the wash-up after Tea![3]

3. Ó Ríordáin, John J.

CHAPTER THIRTEEN

In The New Millennium (2003-2008)
Spailpín fánach

'A Writer of Books'

During our student days in Cluain Mhuire, we had two five-day retreats each year. The men chosen to conduct them were older confrères working on the home or foreign missions. On such occasions, if the speaker quoted a written source he usually acknowledged the author. An exception, however, was Fr John Gorey. Time and again he would quote 'a writer of books' – 'a writer of books remarks,' 'a writer of books tells us.' This became a cant phrase in the folklore of Cluain Mhuire and the phrase is still used jocosely among us even to the present day.

In time, I became a writer of books myself and writing and publishing has gone hand in hand with almost all of my life since ordination. It wasn't that I set out to write because of any conscious love for the art itself. It was a keen awareness that the oral tradition in Ireland was dying. The catalyst that ultimately caused me to put pen to paper was my mother's sudden death on 23 March 1967. With her passing went a lot of family history and genealogical data.

Within a week or two I set about rescuing from oblivion anything of an historical, folkloric, or literary nature that might be of interest to posterity in the region of Kiskeam. Particularly dear to the heart of my mother were the sweet songs and folk traditions of Edward Walsh, a native of the Araglen Valley, known to her grandmother, Nano Casey, at the 'top of the lane' in the Kiskeam of the 1840s as Walsh the Poet. My collection of Walsh material began with two songs received from Dan Seán O'Keeffe of Ruhill and the beginning on that April day came to fruition early in the 21st century. To this we shall return presently.

From first launching out on parish missions in the early 1960s it became evident that the irregular schedules of work were proving incompatible with maintaining an active interest in gardening. A further discovery in 1969 that I had a minor heart ailment meant that climbing mountains, digging the garden and doing any kind of heavy manual work had to be abandoned. Now that my favourite occupations were out of bounds there was more time for folklore collecting.

My first incursion into print was the publication of *Kiskeam And That Way Back*. To call it a book would be a little presumptuous. Nevertheless, this collection of about a hundred pages, rolled off on a Gestetner and stapled, proved highly popular, and even after two further editions in the 1970s the occasional request for it arrives on my desk. Professor Etienne Rynne reviewed it in the *North Munster Archaeological Journal* and the review catapulted it into the public domain. A letter arrived from the acquisitions department of Trinity College, Dublin conveying their unhappiness at not having received a copy of the publication. I didn't respond. They wrote again. The second reminder was not as friendly. 'No reply from the canal end' as Mícheál Ó Hehir used to say. A third letter threatened serious consequences. Having received neither book nor response they next phoned my superior, Stan Mellett, in Limerick, to inform him that he had a lawbreaker in his community. Thinking that he was doing me a favour, Stan told them that the book that so exercised them, was really only a few pages thrown together, and that they were missing nothing. (What a supportive confrère!) Trinity fell silent. When Stan told me how he had rescued me from the jaws of the law, I explained that he had frustrated my design. I was curious to see how far Trinity was prepared to go in pursuit of their legal right.

After *Kiskeam And That Way Back* (1969) came *Kiskeam versus the Empire* in 1972 (Kerryman Edition 1985). If the first title caught the fancy of Trinity, the second hit the *Irish Times*. The subject of the book was the War of Independence in the Kiskeam area, and when people facetiously asked who won, I invariably replied, 'Kiskeam is still there.' Then followed *Irish Catholics, Tradition & Transition* (1980), *Kiskeam Cousins* (1989), *Where Araglen So Gently Flows* (1989), *The Music of What Happens* (1996), *A Pilgrim in Celtic Scotland* (1997), *Irish Catholic Spirituality, Celtic & Roman* (1998), *Early Irish Saints* (2001), *I Primi Santi D'Irlanda, Vitae e Spiritualità* (2005), *A Tragic Troubadour* (2005), and as a new generation had grown up since the days of the 'Empire' and the 'Araglen,' reprints or second editions were sought. For that reason I published a second and enlarged edition of *Where Araglen So Gently Flows* (2007), and who knows what may be done about revisiting *Kiskeam Versus the Empire*.

The course of lectures delivered at Iona Abbey in the Inner Hebrides of Scotland was the basis of my second book on Irish/Celtic Spirituality. Shortly after returning from Iona I was browsing in a Dundalk bookshop and, on seeing what passed for Celtic Spirituality, I said surely we can do better than that. I went back to the monastery, got to work on my texts and the following year The Columba Press, Dublin and St Mary's Press, Winona, USA, released *The Music of What Happens*. Since then The Columba Press has reprinted the work a number of times.

Edward Walsh, A Tragic Troubadour

Although disappointed with my planned sabbatical in Montreal, I didn't let go of the idea of finishing a doctorate. Over the years I had continued to collect any scrap of material on Walsh the Poet until a considerable portfolio had been amassed. Then around the turn of the millennium a number of Walsh-related issues got resolved. I found a collection of his hand-written letters in the manuscript department of the National Library; and after thirty years' exploration finally traced his family, first the dead and then, to my great joy, the living. Edward Walsh's great-great granddaughter, Elizabeth Nunn, was living in Queensland, Australia where her great-great grandmother, Brigid, widow of Edward had settled after her husband's death.

My health was precarious at the time and it was more than likely that in the event of my demise all the research would find its way ignominiously into black plastic bags. With that fear at the back of my mind, I went to see Dr Dáithí Ó hÓgáin in the Folklore Department at Belfield campus and showed him the work done to date. He suggested that we might complete it as a doctoral thesis within six months or so. However, the head of the department insisted that I'd have to be registered at NUI Dublin for a minimum of three years before beginning a thesis. In view of health considerations I decided that apart from the money or the time involved I had the work done and, degree or no degree, I was about to sign off on Edward Walsh.

Back in the monastery, I did some further work on the material, bound it in three volumes and then presented it to Saor Ollscoil na hÉireann saying that if they considered it worthy of a PhD I'd make the necessary adjustments for a formal presentation of the thesis to the university. The authorities examined it, expressed interest in having it presented and within weeks that was accomplished. When they went in search of suitable examiners for the *viva voce* defence, one of the examiners happened to be Dáithí from Belfield, and after an hour and a half at a public defence of the work before Dáithí and Dr Eoghan McAodh, I was awarded a PhD in Liberal Arts.

The award was made for a major work on the poet and folklorist, Edward Walsh (1805-1850). Walsh was, like myself, a native of the Araglen Valley in Western Duhallow, Co Cork. Although largely forgotten now, he was one of our most noted folklore collectors, a composer of many sweet songs, a translator of a considerable body of Jacobite poetry from Irish, and above all was a pioneer, if not the actual originator, of writing Hiberno-English, that is to say, English as spoken in Ireland.

Back On the Old Spot By The River
When I was a boy in the Juvenate, Fr Willie Murphy, also a native of Kiskeam, taught Latin and Greek. Any failure to give the required answers was met with the peremptory instruction, 'the old spot by the river, plaster.' Plaster was a generic appellation especially for defaulters. Being assigned to 'the old spot by the river' meant doing further study of the lesson while kneeling by the nearest classroom wall. For myself in later years 'the old spot by the river' became a synonym for Limerick. It was there that I spent five years in college; it was there that I also spent most of my first two decades as a priest, and it is to Limerick that I returned in the summer of 2003 in the expectation of spending the remainder of my life in that old city defended over three hundred years ago by my direct ancestor Donal a' Chogaidh and his brothers.

Spailpín Fánach
The work of a missioner doesn't get easier with the passage of the years and although I have engaged in an occasional mission

since returning to Munster, my work is mainly in the area of sacramental ministry in our church and doing some lecturing and preaching whenever and wherever the opportunity offers. Early in the new millennium I was invited to give ten lectures twice a year on Irish/Celtic Spirituality in Marianella Pastoral Centre in Dublin. Soon after, an invitation came from our Pastoral Centre in Kinnoull, Perthshire, requesting me to do a similar amount of lecturing on Scottish/Celtic Spirituality. The need for education in the faith is ongoing and my work in the monastery has now developed a pattern of teaching short courses for adults in spring and autumn. And then there is the occasional lecture here and there. Hence, the sub-heading *spailpín fánach*, casual labourer.

After an absence of twenty-nine years, I resumed Sisters' Retreats. In these humbler days, those of us who have survived the post-Vatican II hurricane can sit among the ashes and comfort one another and amazingly, laugh happily. A traditional apostolate of the Redemptorists since the days of St Alphonsus is that of retreats to priests. The number I have given are few and sometimes I wonder if it has anything to do with holding up my dear St Paulinus of Nola, as a model: a model human being, a model priest, a model bishop, and a model married man!

A Mediaeval Journeyman

There has always been a strong romantic streak in my make-up. It's not that I was just fascinated by feminine beauty but by beauty in all spheres, including nature, music, poetry, art. Even when reading St Luke's gospel in public, I sometimes pause with a lump in my throat overwhelmed by the sheer loveliness of the text. In music my tastes are catholic. I have particularly wonderful memories of Wilhelm Kemp in the Savoy in 1965, Virginia Kerr's singing in Kinsale, of a Munster final of Scór in Clonmel in the late 1970s, of hearing Victoria de Los Angeles live at the concert hall in Montreal in 1986 and of Micheál Ó Súilleabháin electrifying the audience with music and song at a concert in aid of renovating the Church of Ireland in Newmarket-on-Fergus in 2007.

An element of melancholy in my personality (somebody once told me that I was like a Goya painting) may account for a certain attraction to Chopin's work. I turn to Mozart when in need of brightening up. A number of Central and Eastern European composers get me into a reflective, prayerful mood. The romanticism in me has something to do with a certain yearning that surfaces again and again, a yearning for the *je ne sais quoi*, ultimately no doubt for God, as Augustine discovered. In more recent years this yearning has not been as acute, and not because of any loss of interest in that which we call God. Perhaps, like Niall Toíbín's story of the Cavan man who used the pedigree bull to do the spring ploughing, life has knocked some of the romance out of me.

Though living in the 21st century, I am perhaps more of a mediaeval man. I find my way of life in spiritual communion with the mediaeval journeymen, holding fellowship with smiths and tinkers, tailors and circus folk, master craftsmen and cathedral builders; troubadours too, and *jongleurs*, musicians and entertainers tramping the mediaeval highways or woodland paths, citizens of the world, bringing news from afar and tales of strange things.

I, too, am a citizen of the world, a journeyman missioner, one of that vast throng of named and nameless itinerant preachers who have wandered far and wide, introducing or fanning the flame of Christian life wherever they went and leaving behind the perfume of the gospel or sometimes traces of clay feet.

In an ever-changing world I find that my prayer, too, is changing. Thanksgiving seems to get more space. Despite all obstacles and almost despite myself, I am what I am, a preacher of the age-old mystery expressed so beautifully by the poet as

a dream born in a herdsman's shed.[1]

From time to time, people refer to me as odd, eccentric, maverick, a *rara avis* or a *fear ann féin*. While not denying the rest of these descriptions I know that I am a *fear ann féin*, no doubt a bit of a mystery to others at times and increasingly, a mystery to myself.

I rarely do the standard things
The conventional is boring –

---

1. Kettle, Thomas, 'To My Daughter Betty, The Gift of God' in Gerald Dawe's *Earth Voices Whispering*, p. 55.

the package tour, the club,
the up-market diner,
and the zoological spectacle
of a box at the theatre.

I pack sandwiches
speed to mountain or shore
lay my table under God's holy heavens
or beneath pine and spreading oak;
Find new life in museums,
Or old graveyards in winter.[2]

2. Ó Ríordáin, John J.

Works Cited

Burns, Robert, *Poems*, Selected and edited by W. Beattie and H. W. Meikle (Penguin Books), 1883.

Dawe, Gerald (ed), *Earth Voices Whispering* (Blackstaff Press) Belfast, 2008.

Kavanagh, Patrick, *The Complete Poems*, (The Goldsmith Press) Newbridge, 1984.

Ó Ríordáin, John J., *Irish Catholics*, (Veritas) Dublin, 1980.

— *A Pilgrim in Celtic Scotland* (Columba Press) Dublin, 1997.

Ryan, Desmond, *The 1916 Poets*, (Gill and Macmillan) Dublin, 1963.

Service, Robert, *Songs of the Sourdough*, (A & C Black) London, 1999.

— *Songs of the High North*, (A & C Black) London, 1999.

— *Collected Verse of Robert Service* (Vol 1) (Ernest Benn Lted) London & Tonbridge, 1960.

Weir, Robert F., *Death in Literature* (Columbia UP) New York, 1980.

'Concilium' 33: The Renewal of Preaching: Theory and Practice (Paulist Press) New York, 1968.